Is It My Armor or God's Armor?

Jewell Probasco

DEDICATION

My utmost admiration and appreciation go to God, our Father in Heaven, for His Inexpressible Gift. My utmost admiration and appreciation go to God, our Lord and Savior, Jesus Christ, for His Unconditional Love, Blood, and Truth. My utmost admiration and appreciation go to God, The Holy Spirit, for His Faithful Revelation and Guidance. That They chose me for this project is outside the reach or the possibility of my understanding, and the honor I feel is beyond the words I have to express.

Acknowledgments

My most profound appreciation to each person who held me up in prayer, faithfulness, and constant support during this endeavor. Many victories would not have been possible without your prayers, love, support, and continual encouragement. As a result, this book has become a realization. Special thanks to my good friends, Rev. Kathy Rivers, who selflessly helped with editing, and Sherry Chance, who has given her graphic talents repeatedly to the blessing of this ministry. What a blessing you all are and continue to be in and to my life.

TABLE OF CONTENTS

INTRODUCTION

"Finally, my brethren, be strong in the Lord and in the power of His might. 11) *Put on the whole armor of God, that you may be able to stand against the wiles of the devil."* (Ephesians 6:10 & 11)

I have heard, as I am sure you have too, numerous Christians, including church leaders and ministers of The Gospel, say, *"Let us put on our armor...."* According to Scripture, The Armor is **NOT** our armor. It is God's Armor.

As Christians, we know that a war is going on around us in the spiritual realm. We can't see it physically because it is invisible nonetheless, it is real, very real. When we were born, we inescapably had an arch-enemy, satan. Our arch-enemy, satan, was and continues to be committed to our defeat and destruction. He is not just the arch-enemy to Christians — satan is the arch-enemy to all of mankind. Mankind is the only creation that looks exactly like God, and satan hates God. He hates us because he sees God's image when he looks at us. Have you ever seen someone that reminded you of a person you were not that fond of? It most likely affected how you acted and felt towards that person until you got to know them for who they are, not who they remind you of. That is the way it is with satan. He sees The God he hates and tries to dethrone Him in our lives when he sees us. You and I are literally hated, loathed, and despised in satan's eyes.

Through Jesus Christ

Through Jesus Christ, we, as God's Children have access to **ALL** The Promises of God written in His Word. For example, The Holy Spirit and The Fruit of The Spirit.

> *"... the fruit of the Spirit is love, joy, peace, longsuffering, kindness, goodness, faithfulness, 23) gentleness, self-control...."* (Galatians 5 22 & 23a)

And so much more. Not only do we have **ALL** The Promises of God that Jesus Christ made Provision for us to have on The Cross at Calvary, but He also gave us eternal life when we believe in Him.

God's Armor Is Not Automatically Put On Us

Does your mother still dress you? Does the pastor dress you? **No!** You must dress yourself, and if you have children, you teach them to do the same.

When we accept Jesus Christ as our Lord and Savior, God's Armor is not automatically put on us. We have to consciously decide to put His Armor on and wear it.

God Alone Is Authority

God Alone Is Authority, and one of the places that He has Established His Authority is in His Armor. We must know and be aware of the fact that we cannot establish our own authority by putting on God's Armor.

If we try to use God's Armor to operate in our own authority, it's called rebellion and a work of our flesh.

> *"So then, those who are in the flesh cannot please God."* (Romans 8:8)

> *"Are ye so foolish? Having begun in the Spirit, are ye now being made perfect by the flesh?"* (Galatians 3:3)

> *"For we are the circumcision, who worship God in the Spirit, rejoice in Christ Jesus, and have no confidence in the flesh."* (Philippians 3:3)

DOES GOD EVER USE US?

If it is my armor, that means God has to use me. Do you like the idea of someone using you? No, of course you don't. I hate it when I feel used by other people. Please take a minute and think about it. I asked The Lord about Him using His children, and He said to me, *"I Love My people too much to use them. However, as it was with Adam in the Garden of Eden before he sinned, and as it was with My Son, Jesus Christ, when He became flesh and lived on the earth, so I still desire to share My Anointing with My children. I Desire My Kingdom to come to this earth through them."* He created us to be and desires us to partner with Him.

I asked Father to take me into His Word and show me where He partnered with a man in Scripture. I had heard the term "Jesus, use me" for so long I couldn't get a clear understanding of what it meant to partner with God. I knew Adam had been created sinless and Jesus

Christ, Father's Son, was born sinless; but how can we, you and I, born into a cursed world, full of sin and unrighteousness, qualify to partner with God and wear His Armor?

God gave us an amazing Principle in the first chapter of Genesis when we read ten times the words, *"And God said...."* God spoke creation, the Universe itself, into existence. Then He created Adam, mankind, in His image, with the same Authority in speech, that He, Himself has — *partnering* with Adam.

From the very beginning, God has shown us that He Loves to partner with mankind. We know that God is Limitless. Yet, God put a limitation on Himself. He chose to allow men to partner and co-labor with Him. Let's take a quick look at what Father shared with me about partnering and co-laboring with Moses and Aaron. Look and listen carefully to the conversation that God is having with Moses.

*"Thus says the Lord: "By this you shall know that I am the Lord. **Behold, I will strike the waters which are in the river with the rod that is in my hand**, and they shall be turned to blood. 18) "And the fish that are in the river shall die, the river shall stink, and the Egyptians will loathe to drink the water of the river." 19) Then the Lord spoke to Moses, "Say to Aaron, '**Take your rod and stretch out your hand** over the waters of Egypt, over their streams, over their rivers, over their ponds, and over all their pools of water, that they may become blood. And there shall be blood throughout all the land of Egypt, both in buckets of wood and pitchers of stone.'" 20) **And Moses and Aaron did so, just as the***

*__Lord commanded. So he lifted up the rod
and struck__ the waters that were in the river, in
the sight of Pharaoh and in the sight of his
servants. And all the waters that were in the river
were turned to blood."* (Exodus 7:17-20 bolding mine)

First, The Lord says the rod is in His hand, *"... I will strike the
waters which are in the river with the rod that is in __my hand__...."*
Next, The Lord told Moses to tell Aaron to take his rod in his hand. *"...
Say to Aaron, 'Take your rod and stretch out __your hand__...."* The
Lord considered His hands to be the same as Moses and Aaron's
hands. He did not "use" Moses and Aaron; He partnered and co-
labored with them. He shared His Anointing and Power with them.
The rod here is symbolic of Authority and Anointing.

Because we now live under The New Covenant, The Covenant of
Grace, God's Authority, and Anointing lives within us. So, that brings
to light a question we must now ask ourselves, "What am I doing with
The Rod — The Authority and Anointing in God's Armor that He has
given me?

GOD'S ARMOR HAS SEVEN PIECES

The Armor of God consists of seven pieces. I have heard it said that
there are only six pieces to His Armor, but six is the number of man.
For example, God made man on the sixth day. Goliath had six fingers
on each hand. He stood six cubits and a span tall. His spearhead
weighed six hundred shekels, and he had a six-piece armor. In
contrast, seven is the number of perfection or completeness. God
made the world in six days, and on the seventh day, He rested.

As you continue to read on, you will learn that each of the seven pieces of God's Armor has a specific meaning and purpose. You will learn what they are, how to apply them, and how they function in your life.

Stand

Against

The

Wiles

Of

The

Devil

STAND AGAINST THE WILES
OF the devil

*"Put on the whole armor of God, that you may be able to **stand** against the wiles of the devil. 12) For we do not wrestle against flesh and blood, but against principalities, against powers, against the rulers of the darkness of this age, against spiritual hosts of wickedness in the heavenly places. 13) Therefore take up the whole armor of God, that you may be able to with**stand** in the evil day, and having done all, to **stand**. 14) **Stand** therefore, having girded your waist with truth, having put on the breastplate of righteousness."* (Ephesians 6:11-14 bolding mine)

Paul mentioned the word *"stand"* four times. When you stand, you do not have to fight. You don't fight. You stand. To stand means that you have already won. We cannot lose battles when we stand in Jesus, dressed in God's Armor. The one left standing after a battle is **ALWAYS THE VICTOR!** God's Desire is for you to be the one left standing. Jesus has given you The Victory!

"<The Father> has delivered and drawn us to Himself out of the control and the dominion of darkness and has transferred us into the kingdom of the Son of His love, 14) In Whom we have our redemption through His blood, <which means> the forgiveness of our sins." (Colossians 1:13 & 14 AMP)

To Stand

From Strong's Concordance is defined as; To cause or make to stand, to place, put, set, to make firm, fix, establish, to uphold or sustain the authority or force of anything, to stop, stand still, to stand immovable, stand firm, stand unharmed, to stand ready or prepared, one who does not hesitate, does not waiver.

Let me use Superman as an example of one who knows how to stand. When Clark Kent (Superman) went to work at the newspaper dressed in his suit and tie, he looked like any other man in the workplace. However, when Clark changed from his suit and tie into his Superman suit, he would stand with his head held high, his shoulders thrown back, his feet firmly planted, hands on his hips, his eyes looking straight ahead set with purpose. He looked confident, strong, courageous, and fearless as he stood there. Likewise, when you and I put on The Armor of God, satan can't see our weaknesses, fears, or lack of courage. To our arch-enemy, satan, we look just like Jesus to him.

I encourage you to stand still, stand firm, stand steadfast. This is the image of you with your head held high, your shoulders thrown back, your feet firmly planted, hands on your hips, and your eyes looking straight ahead set with purpose, confident in your God.

GOD SAYS YOU ARE

Most of us have no trouble believing Who God says He Is. The difficulty comes in believing who He says you are. It is necessary, urgent, vital, crucial, essential, imperative — it cannot be stressed enough that for you to stand, for you to mature, you must believe God's Truth about who He says you are and what you have through Him. Your stability depends on it.

We often see ourselves as losers, but God has no losers in His Kingdom. So, it is crucial that we see ourselves and others as God sees us and treat ourselves and others accordingly.

GOD SAYS WE ARE

God's Child   (John 1:12)

Christ's Friend   (John 15:15)

Bought With A Price   (1 Corinthians 6:20)

A Member Of Christ's Body   (1 Corinthians 12:27)

Established, Anointed, and Sealed By God   (2 Corinthians 1:21 & 22)

Confident Of Father's Perfect Work   (Philippians 1:6)

A Citizen Of Heaven   (Philippians 3:20)

Hidden With Christ In God   (Colossians 3:3)

Born Of God And satan Cannot Touch Me   (1 John 5:18)

Chosen Before The Creation Of The World   (Ephesians 1:4, 11)

Holy and Blameless   (Ephesians 1:4)

Adopted As His Child   (Ephesians 1:5)

Filled With Purpose   (Ephesians 1:9 & 3:11)

Filled With Hope   (Ephesians 1:12)

Sealed With The Promised Holy Spirit   (Ephesians 1:13)

A Saint   (Ephesians 1:18)

The Salt Of The Earth   (Matthew 5:13)

Alive With Christ   (Ephesians 2:5)

Raised Up With Christ   (Ephesians 2:6; Colossians 2:12)

Seated With Christ In Heavenly Places   (Ephesians 2:6)

Living In His Kindness   (Ephesians 2:7)

God's Workmanship   (Ephesians 2:10)

A Member Of God's Household   (Ephesians 2:19)

A Holy Temple   (1 Corinthians 6:19; Ephesians 2:21)

A Dwelling Place For The Holy Spirit   (Ephesians 2:22)

Free To Approach God With Confidence   (Ephesians 3:12)

Victorious   (Galatians 3:13)

A Child Of God   (1 John 5:4)

Crucified With Christ   (Galatians 2:20)

Living In Christ   (Philippians 1:21)

The Apple Of His Eye   (Zechariah 2:8)

The number one tactic of satan is to make you think that you don't have what you already have.

> *"Blessed be the God and Father of our Lord Jesus Christ, who has blessed us with every spiritual blessing in the heavenly places in Christ."*
> (Ephesians 1:3)

satan Is Already Defeated

God does not need you or me to defeat satan because Jesus has already defeated him.

"Having disarmed principalities and powers, He made a public spectacle of them, triumphing over them in it." (Colossians 2:15)

When we begin to affirm ourselves and each other — see ourselves and each other as no better, or no worse, than anyone else and start believing that we will not be shaken, we **WILL** be able to stand because it is God's Truth. Stand in His Truth!

Is It My Armor

or

God's Armor?

Is It My Armor or God's Armor?

"Finally, my brethren, be strong in the Lord and in the power of His might. 11) *Put on the whole armor of God, that you may be able to stand against the wiles of the devil.* 12) *For we do not wrestle against flesh and blood, but against principalities, against powers, against the rulers of the darkness of this age, against spiritual hosts of wickedness in the heavenly places.* 13) *Therefore take up the whole armor of God, that you may be able to withstand in the evil day, and having done all, to stand.* 14) *Stand therefore, having girded your waist with truth, having put on the breastplate of righteousness,* 15) *and having shod your feet with the preparation of the gospel of peace;* 16) *above all, taking the shield of faith with which you will be able to quench all the fiery darts of the wicked one.* 17) *And take the helmet of salvation, and the sword of the Spirit, which is the word of God;* 18) *praying always with all prayer and supplication in the Spirit, being watchful to this end with all perseverance and supplication for all the saints."* (Ephesians 6:10-18)

God tells us through Paul that you are to put on His Armor. As you read on, you will find Jesus wore God's Armor when He walked on this earth. When Jesus returned to Heaven, He lovingly left the Armor that Father had given Him behind for you and me to put on and wear. Therefore, when you put on God's Armor, satan doesn't know who is inside God's Armor. All satan knows is that that was the Armor Jesus Christ was wearing 2,000 years ago when Jesus Christ walked this earth, was Crucified on The Cross at Calvary, and then was Resurrected by The Power of The Holy Spirit, and he, satan, was defeated. As a result of this Victory, you look exactly like Jesus when you are wearing God's Armor. At times you may feel weak, but when you are wearing God's Armor, satan sees you as strong.

EXAMPLE OF WEARING GOD'S ARMOR

My father had been an alcoholic for years. Though he worked and provided a good living for his family (referred to as a working or functioning alcoholic), he was still bound by and addicted to alcohol.

Having made a habit of daily walking and talking with my Lord, Jesus Christ, one day, I felt The Holy Spirit Leading me into spiritual warfare for my father and his deliverance. Thankfully, I was obedient to His Leading. That night I called my mother and father to touch base and check on them. My mother answered the phone, and I asked her how they were doing, and she was excited to tell me, "Your dad has had one of the best days he's had in I don't remember how long. He is laughing, telling jokes, and teasing me, just like he used to do. We have had a Wonderful day!" She also shared that he had not had a drink all day.

When I asked The Lord about what was happening with my father, He explained that my father was **NO LONGER** bound and/or tormented by the spirit of alcoholism. This horrible, foul spirit had bound him for so long that he was not free to make his own choices. The spirit of alcohol had control of him, and he was not free to control his alcohol consumption. Now, because of **THE VICTORY** that had been **WON** through spiritual warfare, my father was free to make his own choices. And, because of God's Grace and Favor, my father never experienced withdrawals of any kind. From that day on, my father was a new man. Did he still drink? Yes, but not daily. Alcohol no longer had control over him. He had control of how much he drank and when to stop. Thank You, Jesus!!!

A POSITION OF AUTHORITY

Wearing The Armor of God places us, as God's Children, in a position of being able to manifest God's Power and Authority in and through our prayers and lives.

It is our duty to strive for a total and complete understanding of God's Armor and how to apply it to our lives. Paul told the Church to *"put on the whole armor of God."* However, before he told them to *"put on the whole armor of God."* He urged them....

- ♦ *"to put away lying"* (Ephesians 4:25)
- ♦ *"to speak truth with your neighbor?"* (4:25)
- ♦ *"be ye angry, and sin not; let not the sun go down upon your wrath."* (4:26)
- ♦ *"neither give place to the devil."* (4:27)
- ♦ *"let him that stole steal no more."* (4:28)
- ♦ *"Let no corrupt communication proceed out of your mouth."* (4:29)
- ♦ *"grieve not the Holy Spirit."* (4:30)
- ♦ *"let all bitterness, and wrath, and anger, and clamour, and evil speaking, be put away from you, with all malice."* (4:31)

As Christians, we must live a consecrated, set apart life and lifestyle as a qualification to wearing God's Armor to be effective in any spiritual warfare we may face.

Our lack of commitment and the secret places of our lives that are not fully surrendered and committed to God will hinder and sometimes stop us dead in our tracks when dealing with satan's attacks.

God has not left us unprotected and vulnerable before our arch-enemy, satan. God has Provided us with His Spiritual Weaponry that can counterattack, overpower, and defeat any design or plan that satan would try to use against us.

I caution you, if you enter into warfare trying to win a battle that Jesus Christ has already won, it is a form of self-righteousness. Your approach has to be one of standing in The Victory that Jesus has already Won.

If you have the attitude that "God has given me the power to defeat the devil." This is a form of pride. God does not need you to defeat satan because satan has **ALREADY** been defeated. Your part is to believe in The Provision that Jesus Christ made for us on The Cross at Calvary and stand in that Victory.

Don't fight for Victory
Fight from Victory

BE

STRONG

IN

THE

LORD

BE STRONG IN THE LORD

*"Finally, my brethren, **be strong in the Lord,** and in the power of His might."* (Ephesians 6:10 bolding mine)

BE STRONG

From Strong's Concordance is defined as; To be strong, endue with strength, receive strength, strengthen, increase in strength, and be bold, headstrong.

When you are *"... strong in the Lord...."* you stagger not at The Promises of God through doubt and unbelief, but you are endued with His Strength, increasing in His Strength as is needed to be bold, resolute, and untiring in His Faith, giving glory to Him.

THE POWER

From Strong's Concordance is defined as; having might, being mighty with great power, dominion, or authority — either delegated or unrestrained, individual power.

MIGHT

From Strong's Concordance is defined as; Ability, force, operative power, an endowment.

We are to open our hearts to receive God's Supernatural Strengthening, an internal deposit of His Power, and His Authority in our inner man.

THE

BELT

OF

TRUTH

THE BELT OF TRUTH

Paul used the armor the Roman soldier wore as a visual example for the Christians at Ephesus that he was writing to, which still applies to all Christians today.

The loin belt was worn around the loins of the Roman soldier. The loins are between the rib and hip bones on both sides of the backbone.

The loin belt was the most essential piece of the Roman soldier's armor. Without it, there was:

- No resting place for his immense shield
- No place to hang his sword
- Nothing for his lance to rest upon
- There was nothing to tack his breastplate down, so it didn't flap in the wind.

The Roman soldier's armor would fall apart if the loin belt were not in place.

Paul mentions the loin Belt of Truth as the first piece of God's Armor. The law of first mention tells us that The Belt of Truth is the essential piece of God's Armor. This shows us that we are to wear Truth as a girdle or belt. We are to equip ourselves with the knowledge of The Truth. When we put God's Belt of Truth around our waist between the rib and hipbone on both sides of the backbone, we stand upright and erect in a fallen world. God's Truth supports our backbone, so we can hold our heads high, with our eyes looking straight ahead to Jesus with purpose, our shoulders thrown back, and our feet firmly planted in and on God's Truth.

*"And you shall know the truth, and the truth shall
make you free."* (John 8:32)

We know that satan comes at us with lies, and if we are not wearing God's Belt of Truth, satan's lies can sound like the truth. We must **ALWAYS** remember what Jesus said of satan,

*"... He was a murderer from the beginning, and
does not stand in the truth, because there is no
truth in him. When he speaks a lie, he speaks from
his own resources, for he is a liar and the father of
it."* (John 8:44b)

Sadly, some Christians do not believe that satan is real. They do not believe that he exists. He does exist. He is real.

GOD IS OMNISCIENT

Some people think satan knows everything. He does not. God is Omniscient, meaning All-Knowing. Consider this; satan did not know that Jesus Christ, our Lord, would gain Victory over him through The Cross at Calvary. The fact is, satan conspired to put Jesus on The Cross. He did not know that Jesus Christ, our Lord, would be Resurrected from the dead after taking back His Authority along with the keys of hell and death from him.

*"I am he that liveth, and was dead; and, behold, I
am alive for evermore, Amen; and have the keys
of hell and of death."* (Revelation 1:18 KJV)

He, satan, would have you believe that he knows everything. But he cannot read your mind. He has no idea what you are thinking until you open your mouth. He can only tell what is going on in your mind and heart by the words that you speak. If you are fearful of something or someone, he doesn't know it until you open your mouth and speak and confess it. This is one of the reasons you are taught to watch your mouth and the confessions you speak.

GOD IS OMNIPOTENT

God is also Omnipotent, meaning All-Powerful. If satan were as all-powerful as some make him out to be, then he would have stopped you from receiving Jesus Christ as your Lord and Savior. He would stop you from attending church services. If he were all-powerful, he would have destroyed and probably killed you long ago.

Scripture tells us that satan is a liar. When Jesus was talking to the Pharisees, He said,

> *"You are of your father the devil, and the desires of your father you want to do. He was a murderer from the beginning, and does not stand in the truth, because there is no truth in him. When he speaks a lie, he speaks from his own resources, for he is a liar and the father of it."* (John 8:44)

Why would satan need to lie if he has all the power he needs to do to us as he pleases? The only power satan has against you is his lies.

People often lie when they don't have the power to make things happen the way they would like. These people lie to give the impression that they have the necessary power needed for whatever they are lying about.

GOD IS OMNIPRESENT

Only God is Omnipresent. Our arch-enemy, satan, would have you believe that he can be everywhere, omnipresent, all the time. But the truth is, satan is a created being and therefore has limitations. He cannot be everywhere all the time attacking anyone he would like to. His principalities, powers, rulers of the darkness of this world, and spiritual wickedness in high places are on assignment by him doing his dirty work for him.

> *"For we wrestle not against flesh and blood, but against principalities, against powers, against the rulers of the darkness of this world, against spiritual wickedness in high places."* (Ephesians 6:12 KJV)

Truth is to deal faithfully or truthfully with anyone and everyone. Truth conforms to reality. Truth is a condition or requirement for service on the part of the followers of Jesus Christ. It is the bracing up of oneself to maintain perfect sincerity and reality as the counteractive in Christian character against hypocrisy and falsehood.

> *"And righteousness shall be the belt of His loins, and faithfulness the belt of His waist."* (Isaiah 11:5)

> *"LORD, who shall abide in thy tabernacle? who shall dwell in thy holy hill? 2) He that walketh*

uprightly, and worketh righteousness, and speaketh the truth in his heart." (Psalms 51:1 & 2)

KEEP YOUR WORD

"In whose eyes a reprobate is despised, but who honors those who fear the LORD; who swears to his own hurt and does not change." (Psalms 51:4 RSV)

In other words, if you, as a child of God, give your word and it proves to be to your disadvantage, you should still keep your word.

"And don't say anything you don't mean. This counsel is embedded deep in our traditions. 34) *You only make things worse when you lay down a smoke screen of pious talk, saying, 'I'll pray for you,' and never doing it, or saying, 'God be with you,' and not meaning it. You don't make your words true by embellishing them with religious lace. In making your speech sound more religious, it becomes less true.* 37) *Just say 'yes' and 'no.' When you manipulate words to get your own way, you go wrong.*" (Matthew 5:33-35 & 37 The Message)

"But let your words be simply, Yes or No: and whatever is more than these is of the Evil One." (Matthew 5:37 BBE)

Jesus Christ Is Truth

Jesus Christ is Truth, and as such, is the most important thing to us.

> *"Jesus said to him, 'I am the way, the truth, and the life. No one comes to the Father except through Me.'"* (John 14:6)

Jesus Christ should live within you at the core of your being. If you take God's Belt of Truth off, you will fall apart. Jesus is Truth. Jesus holds your life together. If you lay truth to the side, you will begin to:

- Lose your sense of Righteousness
- Lose your sense of Peace
- Your Joy will start to diminish
- Your Faith will weaken
- You'll be blown by every wind of doctrine

Without Truth as your support, you will fall apart spiritually.

Protection For Our Reproductive Organs

God's Belt of Truth also protects our reproductive organs. We cannot reproduce unless Truth is operating in our lives. We become sterile spiritually when we don't have Truth operating in our lives. We cannot reproduce. There will be:

- No anointing
- No power
- No strength
- No patience
- No compassion

- No gentleness
- No witness
- No love

Have you ever asked yourself these questions?
- Why is my life such a mess?
- Where did my peace go?
- What should I do?
- Where is the victory?

The Lord is probably asking you in return
- Where is My Belt of Truth I gave you?
- Who took it off you?
- Do you know where you put it?
- When did you take it off?
- How did you lose it?

You find out What and Who Truth is by:
- Developing a love for The Word
- Developing a relationship with our Lord
- Spending time in study and prayer

> *"He who walks uprightly, And works righteousness, and speaks the truth in his heart."* (Psalms 15:2)

> *"Lead me in Your truth, and teach me, For You are the God of my salvation; on You I wait all the day."* (Psalms 25:5)

"All the paths of the LORD are mercy and truth, To such as keep His covenant and His testimonies." (Psalms 25:10)

"For the word of the LORD is right, And all His work is done in truth." (Psalms 33:4)

"Do not withhold Your tender mercies from me, O LORD; let Your lovingkindness and Your truth continually preserve me." (Psalms 40:11)

"Behold, You desire truth in the inward parts, And in the hidden part You will make me to know wisdom." (Psalms 51:6)

"Teach me Your way, O LORD; I will walk in Your truth; unite my heart to fear Your name." (Psalms 86:11)

"He shall cover you with His feathers, And under His wings you shall take refuge; His truth shall be your shield and buckler." (Psalms 91:4)

"I have chosen the way of truth; Your judgments have I laid before me." (Psalms 119:30)

"You are near, O LORD; And all Your commandments are truth." (Psalms 119:151)

"Open the gates, That the righteous nation which keeps the truth may enter in." (Isaiah 26:2)

"And you shall swear, The LORD lives, In truth, in judgment, and in righteousness; The nations shall bless themselves in Him, And in Him shall they glory." (Jeremiah 4:2)

"But the hour is coming, and now is, when the true worshippers shall worship the Father in spirit and in truth: for the Father is seeking such to worship Him." (John 4:23)

"And you shall know the truth, and the truth shall make you free." (John 8:32)

"The Spirit of truth, whom the world cannot receive, because it neither sees Him nor knows Him; but you know Him; for He dwells with you, and will be in you." (John 14:17)

"Rejoiceth not in iniquity, but rejoiceth in the truth." (1 Corinthians 13:6 KJV)

"Who desires all men to be saved and to come to the knowledge of the truth." (1 Timothy 2:4)

"Be diligent to present yourself approved to God, a worker who does not need to be ashamed, rightly dividing the word of truth." (2 Timothy 2:15)

"But the anointing which you have received of Him abides in you, and you do not need that anyone teach you; but as the same anointing teaches you concerning all things, and is true, and is no lie, and just as it has taught you, you will abide in Him." (1 John 2:27)

"I have no greater joy than to hear that my children walk in truth." (3 John 1:4)

"We therefore ought to receive such, that we may become fellow workers for the truth." (3 John 1:8)

If God's Belt of Truth is not in place:

♦ You will not be able to stand.
♦ You will live in confusion.
♦ You will not have any power.
♦ No compassion.
♦ No strength.
♦ No peace.
♦ An ineffective prayer life.
♦ You will be full of unbelief and doubt.
♦ You will lack love for The Written Word.
♦ You will not be an overcomer. You will be overcome.

Strive For God's Knowledge and Understanding

You must strive for God's Knowledge and Understanding. Paul told the Church to *"put on the whole armor of God."* However, before he told them to *"put on the whole armor of God."* He urged them,

- *"putting away lying"* (4:25)
- *"speak truth with his neighbor."* (4:25)
- *"Be angry, and do not sin: do not let the sun go down on your wrath"* (4:26)
- *"nor give place to the devil."* (4:27)
- *"let him that stole steal no longer."* (4:28)
- *"let no corrupt word proceed out of your mouth."* (4:29)
- *"do not grieve the Holy Spirit of God."* (4:30)
- *"Let all bitterness, wrath, anger, clamor, and evil speaking be put away from you, with all malice."* (4:31)

God's Children Are Required To Have A Consecrated, Set-Apart Life

As Christians, we are required by God to have a consecrated, set apart life and lifestyle. Our lack of commitment and the secret places of our lives that are not fully surrendered and given up to God will stop us dead in our tracks when dealing with satan's attacks.

God has not left us unprotected and vulnerable before our arch-enemy, satan. He has Provided us with Spiritual Weaponry through His Armor that can Counterattack, Overpower, and Defeat any design or plan satan would try to use against us.

God's loin Belt of Truth is the piece of God's Armor upon which all the other Armor pieces are held in place. Without Truth, the other pieces of God's Armor will not be secure.

GOD'S

BREASTPLATE

OF

RIGHTEOUSNESS

GOD'S BREASTPLATE
OF RIGHTEOUSNESS

"... having on the breastplate of righteousness."
(Ephesians 6:14b)

The breastplates that the Roman soldiers wore were often so beautiful and striking that it was difficult for people to take their eyes off them. Keeping their breastplates polished and buffed to a magnificent shine, the Roman soldier wore his breastplate with a sense of honor and pride.

The soldier's breastplate began at the top of the neck and went down to the knees. It was made of either bronze or brass, usually brass, and consisted of two different pieces of metal. One piece of metal went down the front, and the other went down the back. These two pieces were held together by solid brass rings on top of the shoulders. History tells us that many of the breastplates the Roman soldiers wore were covered with small-scale-like pieces of metal similar to the scales of a fish.

The breastplate was the heaviest piece of weaponry the Roman soldier wore. Most weighed about 40lbs. However, there are reports of some weighing up to 75lbs. Goliath's breastplate weighed about 125lbs.

As the Roman soldier walked around in his armor, something extraordinary would happen. When two pieces of metal are rubbed together, they begin to add a luster to each other after a while. Where they were shiny in the first place, this rubbing gave them a new glow, causing them to become even shinier.

Imagine a Roman soldier walking toward you on a sunny day with the sun at your back. His breastplate would put off such a glare you could not look at him without shielding your eyes. Their breastplates were used as a defensive weapon. As the Roman soldiers went into battle, the sun's glare from their breastplate would blind their enemy. The same is true for us. When we are wearing God's Breastplate of Righteousness as a defensive weapon, The Glory of God's Holiness, and Righteousness, blinds our arch-enemy, satan.

The Roman soldier's breastplate was also an offensive weapon. It supported and protected the soldier from the enemy's blows as they attacked them. The same is true for us when we put on God's Breastplate of Righteousness. We are protected from satan's blows and attacks.

GOD'S RIGHTEOUSNESS AFFECTS EVERY PART OF YOUR LIFE

God's Righteousness affects your attitudes about yourself. His Righteousness affects every situation in your life and also other people. When you gain an understanding of your righteousness in Christ, it will give you the assurance you need to step out and do The Work of God that He has called you to do.

Evil forces always flee and run from God's Righteousness because they cannot endure The Holy Glory and Brilliance that His Righteousness reflects into their eyes.

You, Will, Become Noticeable To The World Around You

God's Righteousness not only affects the spiritual realm but the natural as well. God's Righteousness will make you noticeable to the world around you.

As you put on God's Breastplate of Righteousness, a righteous consciousness will begin to overtake false emotions of:

♦ Condemnation

♦ Guilt

♦ Shame

♦ Uselessness

♦ Feeling like a failure

♦ Incompetence

♦ Hopelessness

♦ Inferiority

♦ Weakness

♦ Etc.

God's Righteousness not only affects the spiritual realm but the natural as well. God's Righteousness will make you noticeable to the world around you.

As you put on God's Breastplate of Righteousness, a righteous consciousness will begin to overtake false emotions of:

♦ Condemnation

♦ Guilt

♦ Shame

♦ Uselessness

♦ Feeling like a failure

♦ Incompetence

- Hopelessness
- Inferiority
- Weakness
- Etc.

GOD'S

BREASTPLATE

PROTECTS

YOUR

VITAL

ORGANS

YOUR HEART

God's Breastplate of Righteousness protects your heart. If you receive a cut on your arm or leg, chances are you will likely survive. But, if you get stabbed in the heart, you will, in all likelihood, die.

The heart is the organ considered the place of wisdom and governing. The center of rational thoughts and activities. You will find that as you read on, this function is also accredited to the kidneys,

> *"I will bless the LORD, who has given me counsel;*
> *My heart also instructs me in the night seasons."*
> (Psalms 16:7)

When our arch-enemy, satan, attacks you, his goal is to shut down your faith and cause death between you and God. So, he goes after your heart, your spiritual heart, with accusations.

> *"Beloved, if our heart does not condemn us, we*
> *have confidence toward God."* (1 John 3:21)

Let's look at two different scenarios.

FIRST SCENARIO

Your arch-enemy, satan, may say something to you like,
- ♦ You are such a hypocrite.
- ♦ Who do you think you are?
- ♦ Do you call yourself a Christian after what you did?
- ♦ You're a lousy friend.
- ♦ You lost your temper. Why should God give you His Favor?

- ♦ How can you have the nerve to expect good things to happen to you?
- ♦ You know you didn't pray long enough.
- ♦ When was the last time you read your Bible?
- ♦ There you go again, saying the wrong thing.
- ♦ You made a bad choice.
- ♦ Why should God care about you?
- ♦ Etc.

Do any of these accusations sound familiar? With satan, his accusations are **ALWAYS** about what you have or have not done. How you respond to satan's voice of accusation will expose what you believe. How you react to satan's charges is the litmus test of what you believe. This is where the rubber meets the road!

You need to be established in The Righteousness of your Savior, Jesus Christ because it will determine how you respond to the voice of accusation when it comes. The Word states,

> *"For He made Him who knew no sin to be sin for us, that we might become the righteousness of God in Him."* (2 Corinthians 5:21)

However, many Christians respond to satan's accusations with agreeing thoughts such as, *"Yeah, you are right. I don't deserve anything from God. How can I expect God's Favor when my temper flares up as it does?"* This is the response of someone who believes that they need to earn their own righteousness and place of acceptance before God. This person believes that they can expect good from God only when their conduct is good and their own checklist of self-imposed requirements are met.

It is possible to become frustrated and ashamed. You may feel cut off from The Presence of Jesus because of getting angry and thinking you do not qualify to ask for God's Help or His Favor. Some people may even be disappointed with you and reprimand you. You can become even more upset if you blame others for putting you in a foul mood. That is called "Blameshift" it's all **THEIR** fault!

SECOND SCENARIO

Let's look at the difference when you think like this, *"Yeah, satan, you are right. I don't deserve to have God's Favor at all because I lost my temper this morning. But you know what? I am **NOT** looking at what I deserve. I **AM** looking at what Jesus Christ, my Lord, Deserves. Even right now, "Jesus, I thank You that You see me as Perfectly Righteous. Because of The Cross and Your Perfect Sacrifice, I can expect Your Unmerited Favor in my life. Every one of my shortcomings is covered by Your Righteousness. I can expect good, not because I am good, but because Jesus, You are Good! Amen!"*

See the amazing difference? This person is established in The Righteousness of Christ Jesus and not his own right-doing or good behavior. You can live a life depending on The Unmerited Favor of Jesus. Those around you will be impressed by your accomplishment and mark you with their favor and support. Soon, you will begin to experience God's Peace and Joy. You will be feeling and experiencing The Father's Unconditional Love and Favor. Consequently, you become more patient with yourself and others.

Does this mean that you sweep all your failings under the carpet and pretend that they never happened? No way! You will become full of the consciousness that The Lord is with you. You will find the strength in Christ to apologize to whomever you need. You see, a heart that The Unmerited Favor of God has touched cannot hold on to unforgiveness, anger, and bitterness.

Which of the above scenarios demonstrate truth and true holiness? Of course, it is the second one.

> *"Keep your heart with all diligence, For out of it spring the issues of life."* (Proverbs 4:23)

> *"Guard your heart above all else, for it determines the course of your life."* (Proverbs 4:23 NLT)

God's Breastplate of Righteousness will protect your heart by giving you rational thoughts and activities. He will Provide you with His Wisdom and Ability to govern your life.

Your Kidneys

While searching The Holy Scriptures, we find that no other internal organs of the body are mentioned in parallel as often as the heart and the kidneys.

God placed the kidneys in the body lower than the heart. The spiritual connotation of the function of the kidneys is this. The kidneys are considered to be the seat of man's feelings, affections, and passions, as in these verses of joy,

> *"Yea my **reins** shall rejoice, when thy lips speak*
> *right things"* (Proverbs 23:16 KJV bolding mine)

Strong's Concordance reveals that the word ***"reins"*** in Hebrew is kilyah *kil-yaw'* meaning the physical organ of the kidneys. The seat of emotion and affection.

Webster's New Colligate Dictionary links the kidneys to a person's temperament. Jesus said,

> *"I am he which searcheth the **reins** and hearts:*
> *and I will give unto every one of you according to*
> *your works."* (Revelation 2:23b KJV bolding mine)

The word ***reins*** in Greek are also translated as "kidneys" Therefore, a more literal translation of this verse should read,

> *"I am He which searcheth the kidneys and hearts:*
> *and I will give unto every one of you according to*
> *your works."*

*"But, O Lord of hosts, that judgest righteously, that triest the **reins** and the heart, let me see thy vengeance on them: for unto thee have I revealed my cause."* (Jeremiah 11:20 KJV bolding mine)

In the following verse, we read that the heart and kidneys share their position as the site of affections with the heart of grief.

*"Thus my **heart was grieved,** and I was **pricked in my reins.**"* (Psalms 73:21 KJV bolding mine)

The heart and the kidneys are different organs of the body and are in different locations of the body. They have different responses to different motivations; these responses signify something. Thus, such responses could be indicating different qualities that distinguish what sort of person the searched individual is. Jesus, The Searcher of the hearts and kidneys, can interpret such responses and understand the person and what kind of kidney (emotions and affections) they have. David writes,

*"The lines are fallen unto me in pleasant places; yea, I have a goodly heritage. 7) I will bless the LORD, who hath given me counsel: my **reins** also instruct me in the night seasons. 8) I have set the LORD always before me: because he is at my right hand, I shall not be moved."* (Psalms 16:6-8 KJV bolding mine)

How did David's kidneys correct him during the nights when he was awake? If David had had any questions about God's attitude toward him, what sort of person he was, his symbolic spiritual kidneys would give him a correct view of God's Intention toward him. That is why David went on to say:

> *"For You will not leave my soul in Sheol, Nor will You allow Your Holy One to see corruption.* 11) *You will show me the path of life; In Your presence is fullness of joy; At Your right hand are pleasures forevermore."* (Psalms 16:10 & 11)

A DAMAGED, DISEASED, OR INADEQUATE KIDNEY

When a person's kidneys become damaged, diseased, or inadequate, they can go into a coma or unconscious.

If you do not keep your kidneys, emotions, and affections in check and live God's Way, wearing His Breastplate of Righteousness, and living according to His Word, you will lose your sensitivity to who you are in Him. You will become apathetic and unresponsive to God's Presence and what He thinks of you. Your emotions and affections will become defiled and diseased. You will become a person who is full of criticism and dislikes. Your heart will become hardened towards the things of God, and you will fall into indifference and unconsciousness as your relationship with your God falls apart.

YOUR PANCREAS

The pancreas lies behind the stomach and intestines in the upper part of your tummy. It produces hormones that help regulate how your body processes sugar and enzymes that aid digestion. Your pancreas also produces hormones necessary for your body, such as insulin and glucagon.

The pancreas represents your capacity to digest the sweetness of life. Likewise, it is related to intellect, obsession, or mental fixation with perfectionism.

PERFECTIONISM

Perfectionism is not the same as striving to be your best in living and eating healthy or academic growth, as some people may think. All too often, perfectionism is seen as a positive trait that increases a person's chances of success. However, perfectionism can lead to self-defeating thoughts or behaviors that make it harder to achieve goals. It may cause stress, anxiety, depression, and other mental health issues. People who strive for perfection out of feelings of inadequacy or failure are often full of self-criticism.

If your arch-enemy, satan, damages the pancreas, you can feel that you are living in a situation in which someone has betrayed you and/or dishonored you. You can experience resentment that brings you dishonor and shame that causes you fear and disgust. For example, you may think that someone has insulted or disrespected you somehow. You may think, "I cannot believe what they did to me. I didn't expect it. I could never imagine it."

Often these feelings are related to something material, such as an inheritance, a house, a vacation, a salary increase, a settlement, etc.

It could be something you took for granted that you were going to receive, and it does not happen for some reason.

Let's look at an example of a situation from which your arch-enemy, satan, might make you feel bitter or discouraged. *"I see how my spouse insults me every day and makes fun of my background. I feel very disrespected by their total lack of respect for me. They have caused me to separate myself from the joy and sweetness that I expected from them before we were married."*

You may experience anger with life because you don't feel life gives you any "sweet pleasures." So, you decide to reject life, hold onto the anger, and feel imprisoned. You may think that you have come to the end of your rope. So, you choose to stay in place with all the emotions that make you feel helpless because you don't know how to handle them.

You are full of uncertainty. You have lost your energy, physically, mentally, and/or emotionally. You may prefer to give up instead of making an extra effort. Instead of waiting for "sweet pleasures" to come to you, you feel that you are the only one who can offer yourself any joy or peace.

A DAMAGED GENITAL SYSTEM

The pancreas is also known to strongly impact the genital system. A damaged genital system is symbolic of not being able to reproduce for our Lord. A person with their genitals harmed by their arch-enemy, satan, cannot produce for The Kingdom of Heaven by winning souls for Jesus.

"And He said to them, 'Go into all the world and preach the gospel to every creature.'" (Mark 16:15)

This person is unable to reproduce The Fruit of The Spirit.

"But the fruit of the Spirit is love, joy, peace, longsuffering, kindness, goodness, faithfulness, 23) gentleness, self-control. Against such there is no law. 24) And those who are Christ's have crucified the flesh with its passions and desires. 25) If we live in the Spirit, let us also walk in the Spirit."
(Galatians 5:22-25)

WHEN OUR PANCREAS IS PROTECTED AND HEALTHY

When your pancreas is protected and healthy, you understand that the only way you find true purpose in life is to give your life totally over to God and His Purpose for your life. The reason you exist is to serve The One Who made you. Many people try to create their own meaning in life, but this will **ALWAYS** fail. Only The Good and Loving Plans of God will last.

"I will cry to God Most High, To God who accomplishes all things for me. 3) He will send from heaven and save me; He reproaches him who tramples upon me. Selah. God will send forth His lovingkindness and His truth." (Psalms 57: 2 & 3 NAS)

"And we know that all things work together for good to those who love God, to those who are the called according to His purpose." (Romans 8:28)

TRUE FREEDOM

All too many people believe that freedom is doing whatever they would like to do, whenever they would like to do it. On the contrary, The Holy Scriptures teach us that we become a slave to our own desires when we live with no controls.

True freedom is finding and living according to the purpose you were made for. Imagine a freedom that is real inside your mind. It is a freedom that no one can ever take away from you. This is freedom worth having. You find it when you follow Jesus Christ, your Lord, and by wearing His Breastplate of Righteousness.

> *"Therefore if the Son makes you free, you shall be free indeed."* (John 8:36)

> *"Because of Christ and our faith in him, we can now come boldly and confidently into God's presence."* (Ephesians 3:12)

> *"My soul thirsts for God, for the living God. When shall I come and appear before God?"* (Psalms 42:2)

SURROUNDED BY LIGHT, LOVE, AND PEACE

Your arch-enemy, satan, tries to blind you from The Truth that Jesus Christ is Light, Love, and Peace.

> *"In whom the god of this world hath blinded the minds of them which believe not, lest the light of*

the glorious gospel of Christ, who is the image of God, should shine unto them." (2 Corinthians 4:4 KJV)

The goal of your arch-enemy, satan, is to try to turn you away from God. When people do not follow The Ways of God, they turn to the world, a place of sadness, pain, suffering, and hurt.

"For even though they knew God, they did not honor Him as God, or give thanks; but they became futile in their speculations, and their foolish heart was darkened. 22) Professing to be wise, they became fools, 23) and exchanged the glory of the incorruptible God for an image in the form of corruptible man and of birds and four-footed animals and crawling creatures. 24) Therefore God gave them over in the lusts of their hearts to impurity, that their bodies might be dishonored among them. 25) For they exchanged the truth of God for a lie, and worshiped and served the creature rather than the Creator, who is blessed forever. Amen." (Romans 1:21-25 NAS)

Jesus Christ Is Light

"Then Jesus spoke to them again, saying, 'I am the light of the world. He who follows Me shall not walk in darkness, but have the light of life.'" (John 8:12)

"As long as I am in the world, I am the light of the world." (John 9:5)

JESUS CHRIST IS LOVE

"He who does not love does not know God, for God is love." (1 John 4:8)

"And we have known and believed the love that God has for us. God is love, and he who abides in love abides in God, and God in him." (1 John 4:16)

JESUS CHRIST IS PEACE

"For unto us a Child is born, Unto us a Son is given; And the government will be upon His shoulder. And His name will be called Wonderful, Counselor, Mighty God, Everlasting Father, Prince of Peace." (Isaiah 9:6)

"Peace I leave with you, My peace I give to you; not as the world gives do I give to you. Let not your heart be troubled, neither let it be afraid." (John 14:27)

"You will keep him in perfect peace, Whose mind is stayed on You, Because he trusts in You." (Isaiah 26:3)

Wearing God's Breastplate of Righteousness guarantees to us, His Sweetness of life.

YOUR RIBS

The most famous rib in The Word of God is the rib God took from Adam's side and formed into Eve in the Garden of Eden.

> *"And the LORD God caused a deep sleep to fall on Adam, and he slept; and He took one of his ribs, and closed up the flesh in its place. 22) Then the rib which the LORD God had taken from man He made into a woman, and He brought her to the man."* (Genesis 2:21 & 22)

We have heard it said that God did not take Eve from his feet to walk on her. He did not take Eve from his head so that he could lord over her. God took Eve from his side because she was to be his equal.

As equals, Adam and Eve had no sense that their lives were their own. They lived as one. They experienced all life, thoughts, and emotions flowing to them from God until the fall. Adam and Eve lacked the capacity to separate their hearts and their minds. They could not desire one thing and use their minds to choose another; their minds followed their hearts. Because their lives were totally centered on God.

Adam did not know that he had a need. God saw that he had a need, representing that Adam was okay with being on his own. A part of every person feels their life is their own. Their thoughts are their own. Their feelings are their own. This is not the way God intended for us to live. Because all life comes from The LORD does not mean that we don't have our own personalities, dispositions, and behaviors. It means that God intended for us to live God-centered.

OUR RIBS PROTECT US

The primary purpose of our rib cage is protection. The rib cage is the core portion of our bodies, enclosing the heart and protecting the lungs. Our rib cage surrounds the chest and heart cavity. The rib cage is also a part of our respiratory system. Our breathing is made possible as the lungs expand and contract. God created us so that the diaphragm has elastic recoil of the rib cage. The lungs take in air then expel that air. The ribs enable our bodies to breathe and have life.

There is no other bone in the human body that compares to the ribs. It is possible that God chose Adam's rib to symbolize the importance of the female to every marriage. For example, I have been a wife, and I am a mother. As such, I discovered that the woman breathes life into her marriage and family. The woman kisses away the pain of her children and her husband. She breathes on the hurts, injuries, and discomforts to help make the pain go away. She is the breath of life to every home. Her husband should be captured by her love as they become one. A husband is moved by the love of his wife as her strength in love captures and guards his heart, breathes life into their marriage, and is the center and core of that love.

> *"... He who made them at the beginning 'made them male and female,'* 5) *and said, 'For this reason a man shall leave his father and mother and be joined to his wife, and the two shall become one flesh?'"* (Matthew 19:4 & 5)

A husband and wife are to be considered one body. God's Plan is for two souls to become one, their two spirits to become interwoven — with a complete blending of interests, an indissoluble partnership of life and fortune, comfort and support, desires and inclinations, joys and sorrows. It is a mistake to consider husband and wife as two separate beings. They are two halves of a single form, two different halves that fit tightly together to make one. They are life and love portrayed in flesh and blood in holy union.

Even as a man and woman are one flesh and members of each other's body, we too are members of the body of Christ.

> *"So husbands ought to love their own wives as their own bodies; he who loves his wife loves himself.* 29) *For no one ever hated his own flesh, but nourishes and cherishes it, just as the Lord does the church.* 30) *For we are members of His body, of His flesh and of His bones."* (Ephesians 5:28-30)

We know that every person has inherited the sinful nature of Adam. However, we can become reconciled to God through believing in Jesus Christ and His Grace. He Is The Head of the church and The Savior of the body of the church. We who have been born again are united with Jesus Christ as one, even as Adam and Eve were one. We are united to Him in the closest way possible. Similar to that relationship between Adam and Eve.

> *"For we are members of His body, of His flesh and of His bones."* (Ephesians 5:30)

God means for you to be in a wonderful, pure, and permanent holy union with Him.

When your rib cage becomes damaged by your arch-enemy, satan, you isolate yourself. You consider only your own feelings in situations. This is selfishness, and selfishness is a form of pride and self-righteousness.

When we are wearing God's Breastplate of Righteousness, everyone is our equal. There is no big me and little you. We must become one with others for God's Breastplate of Righteousness to have its full effect in our lives. Putting on and wearing God's Breastplate of Righteousness will cause us to sacrifice for others and be a blessing to others.

If your ribs, symbolic of your relationships with others, are injured, you can become limp or lame. It becomes difficult to sit still and give someone your full attention. You are unable to stand with your back straight. When you are unable to stand up straight, it means you've lost your confidence. You become shut off to others, tempted to isolate yourself. It may become difficult to be candid and vulnerable with others. And you are unable to breathe deeply with injured ribs. You will not be able to be at peace and rest in God's Presence. You are not able to breathe in and enjoy His Unconditional Love, His Revelation, His Purpose for your life. Injured or broken ribs will affect every part of your body.

Your Lungs

Breathing is a Miracle we don't stop to think about very much. It's involuntary; we automatically do it. Our lungs relax and expand thousands of times every day to get the oxygen we need. When our lungs use that oxygen, we expel that air out of our lungs. It becomes carbon dioxide.

> *"And the LORD God formed man of the dust of the ground, and breathed into his nostrils the breath of life; and man became a living being."* (Genesis 2:7)

> *"The Spirit of God has made me, And the breath of the Almighty gives me life?* (Job 4:33)

Our lungs are the largest organ in our bodies that have contact with the world. Our lungs have an internal surface area of some 753.47373 square feet, while the skin surface only covers 16.145866 to 21.527821 square feet

With our skin, we have the choice of touching other people (or things) or leaving them alone, while the contact we introduce through our lungs is indirect and largely unconscious, which is mandatory. We cannot prevent it, even when things happen that give the reaction of 'taking our breath away.'

SPIRITUAL BREATHING

In the same way, God Created us with the capacity to breathe to sustain our natural lives, He has given us a way to "breathe spiritually" for our spiritual well-being.

Spiritual breathing, like physical breathing, is a process of inhaling the pure things of God and exhaling the impure things of this world. Spiritual breathing is an exercise in faith that enables a Christian to experience God's Unconditional Love and Forgiveness and walk in The Spirit as a way of life.

Sadly, most Christians do not understand the concept of spiritual breathing as an exercise of faith and, as a result, live on what I will refer to as a "spiritual roller coaster." These people go from one emotional experience to another, living most of their life as a worldly Christian, running their own lives, frustrated and fruitless.

We don't usually think about our physical breathing because God created us so that breathing comes naturally without giving it any thought. But spiritual breathing is something that requires a conscious action — a readiness to "inhale" (trust God to fill us with The Holy Spirit) and to "exhale" (confess our sin).

"Spiritual exhaling" is returning wholeheartedly to God, agreeing with Him about our sin, whether in thought or deed, thanking Him for His Forgiveness, and trusting Him to transform our attitudes and actions as we walk in obedience to Him.

Confessing our sin is the key to a peaceful life. If you don't readily acknowledge the sin, it will pull you down and eat you up. Spiritual breathing helps you stick close to God, live in His Presence with Him moment by moment, and remain conscious of His Unconditional Love for you.

How Do I Confess?

How do you confess? Here's an example. *"Father, I confess to You that I did _____________ (name the sin). I admit that I was wrong for _____________ (name the sin), and I am sorry. Father, I am so thankful that Jesus Christ, Your Son, took all my sin past, present, and future upon Himself on The Cross at Calvary and by Sacrificing Himself bore The Ultimate Judgement for my sin. Thank You that The Precious Blood of Jesus covers my sin. I choose to believe what Jesus did for me and accept Your Forgiveness. I ask for Your Help so that I do not repeat this sin against You ever again. If I start to fail, Holy Spirit, would You please remind me of my commitment to You. Thank You."*

How To Inhale Spiritually

To inhale spiritually is to receive The Fullness of The Holy Spirit by faith. How do you do that?

When you receive Jesus Christ as your Lord, Savior, Forgiver, and Leader, The Holy Spirit immediately enters your life, and He never leaves.

> *"But as many as received Him, to them He gave the right to become children of God, to those who believe in His name."* (John 1:12)

> *"For in Him dwells all the fullness of the Godhead bodily;* 10) *and you are complete in Him, who is the head of all principality and power."* (Colossians 2:9 & 10)

"And I will pray the Father, and He will give you another Helper, that He may abide with you forever 17) the Spirit of truth, whom the world cannot receive, because it neither sees Him nor knows Him; but you know Him, for He dwells with you and will be in you." (John 14:16 & 17)

"Awake to righteousness, and sin not...." (1 Corinthians 15:34a KJV)

The more you *"awake"* to the fact that you are The Righteousness of God in Christ, you are Righteous apart from your works, the more you are empowered to live a life that brings Glory to God.

THE FRUIT OF THE SPIRIT

The Holy Spirit lives in you so that you can demonstrate The Fruit of The Spirit and become more like Christ.

"But the fruit of the Spirit is love, joy, peace, longsuffering, kindness, goodness, faithfulness, 23) gentleness, self-control...." (Galatians 5:22-23a)

"And do not be conformed to this world, but be transformed by the renewing of your mind, that you may prove what is that good and acceptable and perfect will of God." (Romans 12:2)

"But we all, with unveiled face, beholding as in a mirror the glory of the Lord, are being

transformed into the same image from glory to glory, just as by the Spirit of the Lord." (2 Corinthians 3:18)

Experience a meaningful prayer life and study of God's Word.

"... that men always ought to pray and not lose heart." (Luke 18:1)

"Likewise the Spirit also helps in our weaknesses. For we do not know what we should pray for as we ought, but the Spirit Himself makes intercession for us with groanings which cannot be uttered." (Romans 8:26)

EXPERIENCE HIS POWER IN WITNESSING

"But you shall receive power when the Holy Spirit has come upon you; and you shall be witnesses to Me in Jerusalem, and in all Judea and Samaria, and to the end of the earth." (Acts 1:8)

BE PREPARED FOR SPIRITUAL BATTLE AGAINST THE WORLD, THE FLESH, AND satan

"Do not love the world or the things in the world. If anyone loves the world, the love of the Father is not in him. 16) For all that is in the world — the lust of the flesh, the lust of the eyes, and the pride of life — is not of the Father but is of the world. 17)

*And the world is passing away, and the lust of it;
but he who does the will of God abides forever."* (1
John 2:15-17)

*"I say then: Walk in the Spirit, and you shall not
fulfill the lust of the flesh.* 17) *For the flesh lusts
against the Spirit, and the Spirit against the flesh;
and these are contrary to one another, so that you
do not do the things that you wish."* (Galatians 5:16 &
17)

*"Casting all your care upon Him, for He cares for
you.* 8) *Be sober, be vigilant; because your
adversary the devil walks about like a roaring
lion, seeking whom he may devour.* 9) *Resist him,
steadfast in the faith, knowing that the same
sufferings are experienced by your brotherhood in
the world."* (1 Peter 5:7-9)

*"Finally, my brethren, be strong in the Lord and
in the power of His might.* 11) *Put on the whole
armor of God, that you may be able to stand
against the wiles of the devil.* 12) *For we do not
wrestle against flesh and blood, but against
principalities, against powers, against the rulers
of the darkness of this age, against spiritual hosts
of wickedness in the heavenly places.* 13) *Therefore
take up the whole armor of God, that you may be
able to withstand in the evil day, and having done*

all, to stand. 14) Stand therefore, having done all, to stand." (Ephesians 6:10-13)

EXPERIENCE POWER TO RESIST TEMPTATION AND SIN

"No temptation has overtaken you except such as is common to man; but God is faithful, who will not allow you to be tempted beyond what you are able, but with the temptation will also make the way of escape, that you may be able to bear it." (1 Corinthians 10:13)

"I can do all things through Christ who strengthens me." (Philippians 4:13)

"And what is the exceeding greatness of His power toward us who believe, according to the working of His mighty power 20) which He worked in Christ when He raised Him from the dead and seated Him at His right hand in the heavenly places, 21) far above all principality and power and might and dominion, and every name that is named, not only in this age but also in that which is to come. 22) And He put all things under His feet, and gave Him to be head over all things to the church, 23) which is His body, the fullness of Him who fills all in all." (Ephesians 1:19-23)

"For God has not given us a spirit of fear, but of power and of love and of a sound mind." (2 Timothy 1:7)

Though all born-again Christians have The Holy Spirit living inside them, not all are filled with The Holy Spirit. Not all are experiencing what He has to offer.

To be filled — empowered and controlled — by The Holy Spirit, we must, in faith, acknowledge our dependence on Him and give Him the control of our life.

"... be filled with the Holy Spirit." (Ephesians 5:18)

GOD'S BREASTPLATE OF RIGHTEOUSNESS PROTECTS OUR LUNGS

Someone once said, *"In sadness, we breathe heavy sighs. In joy, our lungs feel almost like they will burst. In fear, we hold our breath and have to be told to breathe slowly to help us calm down. When we're about to do something hard, we take a deep breath to find our courage."*

Spiritual causes of damaged lungs or lung disease refer to depression, mourning, fear of living, etc. Sadly, these people are denying life. They have been emotionally hurt and no longer allow healing. Sadly, if things don't change for them, they may die because they refuse life and healing.

Some results of unprotected lungs by God's Breastplate of Righteousness will suffer:

- ◆ Emotional hurt
- ◆ Unhappiness

- ◆ Rejection
- ◆ A sense of giving up
- ◆ Fear of living life fully
- ◆ Depression
- ◆ Mourning
- ◆ Hopelessness
- ◆ Feelings of unworthiness
- ◆ Fear of being controlled
- ◆ People pleasers

Some experience panic attacks with hyperventilation or over-breathing. If things don't change for these people, they may die because too many refuse life and healing.

BREATHING BOTH SPIRITUALLY AND PHYSICALLY

Breathing both spiritually and physically is the process by which your body is being charged with energy, life, and love. If God's Breastplate of Righteousness does not cover your lungs, they can be penetrated. If you cannot breathe, every organ in your body will eventually shut down and die. It will become difficult for you to think or talk effectively.

When wearing God's Breastplate of Righteousness, He Protects us and Prevents our arch-enemy, satan, from damaging or destroying our lungs.

THE STOMACH

Your stomach is located in the upper-left area of your abdomen below your liver and next to the spleen. Its principal function is to store and break down the foods and liquids you eat and drink. Then your stomach prepares the food and liquids to be distributed into the various part of your body for its nourishment.

The stomach has been called the seat of hunger. When our stomachs feel empty, there is a lack of food. It is also called the seat of our mental faculties. This refers to the hunger we experience for the things of God. We feel empty when there is a lack of spiritual food.

PHYSICAL HUNGER

> *"So He humbled you, allowed you to hunger, and fed you with manna which you did not know nor did your fathers know, that He might make you know that man shall not live by bread alone; but man lives by every word that proceeds from the mouth of the LORD."* (Deuteronomy 8:3)

SPIRITUAL HUNGER

> *"Blessed are those who hunger and thirst for righteousness, For they shall be filled."* (Mathew 5:6)

> *"You are my God; Early will I seek You; My soul thirsts for You; My flesh longs for You In a dry and thirsty land Where there is no water."* (Psalms 63:1)

"My soul shall be satisfied as with marrow and fatness, And my mouth shall praise You with joyful lips." (Psalms 63:5)

"For He satisfies the longing soul, And fills the hungry soul with goodness." (Psalms 107:9)

"Behold, the days are coming," says the Lord GOD, "That I will send a famine on the land, Not a famine of bread, Nor a thirst for water, But of hearing the words of the LORD." (Amos 8:11)

"And Jesus said to them, 'I am the bread of life. He who comes to Me shall never hunger, and he who believes in Me shall never thirst.'" (John 6:35)

"As newborn babes, desire the pure milk of the word, that you may grow thereby, 3) if indeed you have tasted that the Lord is gracious." (1 Peter 2:2 & 3)

MENTAL SENSES

Additionally, the stomach is symbolic of your level of sensitivity. It symbolizes how well you can "stomach" or accept something. For example: How sensitive are you when having your feelings hurt or when you allow something to upset you?

STOMACH AS A SYMBOL OF INNER THOUGHTS

"The words of a talebearer are like tasty trifles, And they go down into the inmost body." (Proverbs 18:8)

"So I went to the angel and said to him, 'Give me the little book.' And he said to me, 'Take and eat it; and it will make your stomach bitter, but it will be as sweet as honey in your mouth.'" (Revelation 10:9 & 10)

STOMACH AS A SYMBOL OF WORLDLINESS

"Whose end is destruction, whose god is their belly, and whose glory is in their shame — who set their mind on earthly things." (Philippians 3:19)

"For those who are such do not serve our Lord Jesus Christ, but their own belly, and by smooth words and flattering speech deceive the hearts of the simple." (Romans 16:18)

CRAWLING ON ONE'S STOMACH IS A SIGN OF SUBMISSION

Part of God's curse upon satan.

"So the LORD God said to the serpent: 'Because you have done this, You are cursed more than all cattle, And more than every beast of the field; On

your belly you shall go, And you shall eat dust All the days of your life.'" (Genesis 3:14)

Submission as it applies to you and me as God's child.

"Those who dwell in the wilderness will bow before Him, And His enemies will lick the dust." (Psalms 72:9)
"Kings shall be your foster fathers, And their queens your nursing mothers; They shall bow down to you with their faces to the earth, And lick up the dust of your feet. Then you will know that I am the LORD, For they shall not be ashamed who wait for Me." (Isaiah 49:23)

"The wolf and the lamb shall feed together, The lion shall eat straw like the ox, And dust shall be the serpent's food. They shall not hurt nor destroy in all My holy mountain," Says the LORD. " (Isaiah 65:25)

"They shall lick the dust like a serpent; They shall crawl from their holes like snakes of the earth. They shall be afraid of the LORD our God, And shall fear because of You." (Micah 7:17)

EXAMPLES OF THE STOMACH

INCLINATION AND/OR LIKING

A person who has no stomach to fight will turn and walk away.

ANGER AND/OR VIOLENCE OF TEMPER

This person's look is stern, full of self-importance and arrogance. If you do not react or respond in the way they think you should, they get angry and, sadly, all too often violent.

MOODINESS

This person is changeable. One minute they are happy. The next, they are grumpy. You seem to have to walk gently around them because you are never sure of their reactions to what you may say or do.

RESENTMENT

This person often suffers from anger, bitterness, and hostility. They usually have a tendency to cry, trying to achieve sympathy or empathy from another person — this sort of crying proceeds from pride.

This person can be willful, persistent, and stubborn. They think they know where the fault lies. They feel that the other person must change their direction and/or thinking.

PRIDE AND HAUGHTINESS

Pride and arrogance cause people to think too highly of themselves — a know-it-all.

RESENT OR TO REMEMBER WITH ANGER

What is referred to as having a "stomachful." A feeling of having had enough. Willfully contradictory, unreasonable, and rebellious.

NOT DIGESTING GOD'S WORD CORRECTLY

Too many Christians struggle with whether or not they deserve to be Blessed, Favored, and/or Victorious in their life as The Scriptures tell us we should be.

Let me ask you this: does **Jesus** deserve to be Blessed, Favored, and Victorious? Yes. Living a Blessed life and having a Blessed Future **IS NOT** contingent upon how much you strive to be perfect or how hard you work at changing yourself. It is contingent on The Person of Jesus Christ, our Lord.

When wearing God's Breastplate of Righteousness, you are wearing God's Righteousness.

> *"For if by the one man's offense death reigned through the one, much more those who receive abundance of grace and of the gift of righteousness will reign in life through the One, Jesus Christ."* (Romans 5:17)

God's Word Proclaims,

"... as He is, so are we in this world" (1 John 4:17)

Does Jesus Deserve to be Blessed, Favored, and Victorious? Then so do you! This is what being **IN** Christ Jesus means. It means that today, God assesses you and sees you based on The Perfection of Jesus Christ through The Cross at Calvary. God's Word explains that because Jesus, Who knew no sin, became sin for us, we are now The Righteousness of God in Christ. Jesus Christ is your Righteousness.

"For He made Him who knew no sin to be sin for us, that we might become the righteousness of God in Him." (2 Corinthians 5:21)

"Righteousness" is a legal term. It means to have right standing before God. Vine's Expository Dictionary of Biblical Words defines righteousness as, *"That gracious gift of God to men whereby all who believe on The Lord Jesus Christ are brought into right relationship with God."* So, you see, your right standing before God is based upon The Right Standing of Jesus before God.

You are as Righteous as Jesus Is because your Righteousness is from Him. His Righteousness is something you can never obtain or achieve through your right doing; it can only be received by your right believing in Jesus. When you accepted Jesus Christ as your Lord and Savior, He took away all your unrighteousness once and for all and gave you His Gift of Righteousness. Our Lord, Jesus Christ, Purchased it for you on The Cross at Calvary.

When you receive God's Gift of Righteousness, The Word declares that….

"... those who receive abundance of grace and of the gift of righteousness will reign in life through the One, Jesus Christ" (Romans 5:17 bolding mine)

When you eat and fill yourself upon God's Word and wear God's Breastplate of Righteousness, you will reign in life. When you reign in life, fear, depression, and every obstacle that has ever obstructed you from living your life to the fullest will be torn down and flushed out! Your temper, resentments, hurts, wounds, pridefulness, and addictions are not flushed out.

On the other hand, if you are not wearing God's Breastplate of Righteousness, your arch-enemy, satan, will affect both your physical and spiritual digestion. Your stomach will be penetrated, and you will not be able to digest God's Word correctly. As a result, you will become confused and easily deceived.

THE BOWELS

The bowels are located below the stomach. The Word describes our bowels as the seat of tender mercies, kindness, humbleness of mind, meekness, and longsuffering.

"For God is my record, how greatly I long after you all in the bowels of Jesus Christ." (Philippians 1:8 KJV)

"If there be therefore any consolation in Christ, if any comfort of love, if any fellowship of the Spirit, if any bowels and mercies." (Philippians 2:1 KJV)

"Put on therefore, as the elect of God, holy and beloved, bowels of mercies, kindness, humbleness of mind, meekness, longsuffering." (Colossians 3:12 KJV)

We also find in The Word that bowels describe feelings of distress and sorrow.

"My bowels boiled, and rested not: the days of affliction prevented me." (Job 30:27 KJV)

"Behold, O LORD; for I am in distress: my bowels are troubled; mine heart is turned within me; for I have grievously rebelled: abroad the sword bereaveth, at home there is as death." (Lamentations 1:20 KJV)

"Mine eyes do fail with tears, my bowels are troubled, my liver is poured upon the earth, for the destruction of the daughter of my people; because the children and the sucklings swoon in the streets of the city." (Lamentations 2:11 KJV)

"By thee have I been holden up from the womb: thou art he that took me out of my mother's bowels: my praise shall be continually of thee."
(Psalms 71:6 KJV)

If you do not have on God's Breastplate of Righteousness, satan will penetrate your bowels and....

INSTEAD OF HAVING	YOU WILL BE
tender mercies	abrasive and cruel
kindness	unkind and spiteful
humbleness of mind	arrogant and self-centered
meekness	aggressive and belligerent
longsuffering	intolerant and narrow-minded

If your arch-enemy, satan, impairs your bowels, it will affect your willpower and courage. You will lose your resolve. Standing up in today's world as a Christian takes willpower, courage, steadfastness, and resolve.

Wearing God's Breastplate of Righteousness imparts to you God's Willpower, Courage, Steadfastness, and Resolve.

THE SPLEEN

The spleen is located on the left side of the body, just under the rib cage and to the left of the stomach and pancreas. Though your spleen is well-protected, a hard blow to the left side can break ribs which could rupture the spleen and cause massive internal bleeding.

Physically, the spleen is the organ that produces and cleans the body's blood.

Spiritually, the spleen is symbolic of feelings of anger, having a bad temper, being disagreeable, and being hard to get along with. There is an expression "venting my spleen." This means when a person vents at person X — person X is the focus of their anger. Feelings of anger and disagreement manifest in various ways, such as shouting at people, throwing objects, or even being emotionally and physically abusive.

AN EXAMPLE OF ANGER IN THE WORD

When Rebekah heard of the anger Esau had toward Jacob, she said….

> *"Surely your brother Esau comforts himself concerning you by intending to kill you.* 43) *"Now therefore, my son, obey my voice: arise, flee to my brother Laban in Haran.* 44) *'And stay with him a few days, until your brother's fury turns away,* 45) *'until your brother's anger turns away from you, and he forgets what you have done to him; then I will send and bring you from there. Why should I*

be bereaved also of you both in one day?" (Genesis 25:42 - 45)

Rebekah was so concerned about Esau's temper that she feared for her son, Jacob's safety, and perhaps even his life. His fear was so great that she was willing to send him away.

> *"Let all bitterness, wrath, anger, clamor, and evil speaking be put away from you, with all malice."* (Ephesians 4:31)

> *"But now you yourselves are to put off all these: anger, wrath, malice, blasphemy, filthy language out of your mouth."* (Colossians 3:8)

> *"Be angry, and do not sin": do not let the sun go down on your wrath."* (Ephesians 4:26)

Sadly, some Christians feel like God is angry with them for losing their temper or having feelings of disagreement. When a person feels like God is angry at them, it causes feelings of insecurity, uncertainty, shame, and worthlessness, and these feelings cause hopelessness to set in.

GOD, OUR FATHER, IS NOT ANGRY

When you think that The Father is angry or displeased with you, you will not feel confident of or in His Unconditional Love for you. Instead, you will feel condemned and expect and fear punishment from Him. As a result, you stay away from Him because you fear His Anger.

The truth is, Father is not angry with you, even when you fail or blow it. As The Word says, all your sins have already been judged in the body of His Son, Jesus Christ, on The Cross at Calvary.

There is a law called, 'The Law of Double Jeopardy." This law states that the same crime cannot be tried twice. Therefore, The Fire of God's Anger will never fall on you as a believer because it has already fallen on His Son, Jesus Christ, on The Cross at Calvary. The Father judged all the sins of the world at that time.

Does that mean it is okay for you to lose your temper, argue, or physically abuse someone? **No, It Does Not**. You will see others differently when you wear God's Breastplate of Righteousness. God's Love, Compassion, Empathy, and so on, becomes your lifestyle. You will find that you have a tolerance for others and their thoughts and opinions that you never had before. Your life becomes all about Jesus and living your life His Way, not about your selfish thoughts and/or ideas.

Our Father is **NOT** out to judge us but to Bless us. Not because we deserve it, but because Jesus Christ, His Son, our Lord, was Judged and Punished in our place!

satan CAN NO LONGER GO BEFORE GOD AND ACCUSE YOU

The book of Job tells us that satan came before God's Throne and complained about Job.

> *"Now there was a day when the sons of God came*
> *to present themselves before the LORD, and Satan*
> *also came among them. 7) And the LORD said to*
> *Satan, 'From where do you come?' So Satan*

*answered the L*ORD *and said, 'From going to and fro on the earth, and from walking back and forth on it.' 8) Then the L*ORD *said to Satan, 'Have you considered My servant Job, that there is none like him on the earth, a blameless and upright man, one who fears God and shuns evil?' 9) So Satan answered the L*ORD *and said, 'Does Job fear God for nothing? 10) Have You not made a hedge around him, around his household, and around all that he has on every side? You have blessed the work of his hands, and his possessions have increased in the land. 11) But now, stretch out Your hand and touch all that he has, and he will surely curse You to Your face!' 12) And the L*ORD *said to Satan, 'Behold, all that he has is in your power; only do not lay a hand on his person.' So Satan went out from the presence of the L*ORD."*
(Job 1:6–12)

We know that God's Throne is The Most Holy Place. So, why did God allow satan to come before Him? Our arch-enemy, satan, could go before God because Adam had given up his place of authority and his ability to stand before God's Throne in The Most Holy Place when he bowed his knee to satan in the Garden of Eden. (Genesis 3)

Now, under The New Covenant of Grace, Jesus, the last Adam, has come! And the sprinkling of His Blood has cleansed the things of Heaven where satan once stood.

"<In fact> under the Law almost everything is purified by means of blood, and without the

shedding of blood there is neither release from sin and its guilt nor the remission of the due and merited punishment for sins. 23) *By such means, therefore, it was necessary for the <earthly> copies of the heavenly things to be purified, but the actual heavenly things themselves <required far> better and nobler sacrifices than these.* 24) *For Christ* (the Messiah) *has not entered into a sanctuary made with <human> hands, only a copy and pattern and type of the true one, but <He has entered> into heaven itself, now to appear in the <very> presence of God on our behalf."* (Hebrews 9:22–24 AMP)

The Blood that Jesus Christ shed on The Cross at Calvary has Cleansed and Redeemed the unclean place before God's Throne where satan walked and stood before God. Therefore, there remains no place in Heaven for satan, your arch-enemy, to go before God to accuse you.

Who, then, is in God's Presence today? Jesus Christ, our Lord, is! He is there.

"For Christ (the Messiah) *has not entered into a sanctuary made with <human> hands, only a copy and pattern and type of the true one, but <He has entered> into heaven itself, now to appear in the <very> presence of God on our behalf."* (Hebrews 9:24 AMP)

Since Jesus Is For You

> *"Who would dare even to point a finger? The One
> who died for us — who was raised to life for us! —
> is in the presence of God at this very moment
> sticking up for us."* (Romans 8:34 The Message)

What happened to Job cannot happen to you or me. Job longed for a mediator or arbitrator, but he had none.

> *"How I wish we had an arbitrator to step in and
> let me get on with life."* (Job 9:33)

His wish, his longing, is our reality. Today, we have Jesus Christ as our Mediator and Arbitrator ever making intercession for us!

> *"For there is one God and one Mediator between
> God and men, the Man Christ Jesus."* (1 Timothy 2:5)

Since our arch-enemy, satan, cannot come before God anymore, he comes to you here on earth and accuses you in your conscience. His greatest tool is deception because he has no real power. Jesus took care of that too.

Discouragement – satan's Best Tool

It was once announced that the devil was going out of business and would offer all his tools for sale to whomever would pay his price. On the night of the sale, the tools were all attractively displayed, and a bad-looking lot they were. Malice, hatred, envy, jealousy, sensuality, deceit, and all the other implements of evil were spread out, each marked with its price. Apart from the rest lay a harmless-looking wedge-shaped tool, much worn and priced higher than any of them.

Someone asked the devil what it was. "That's discouragement," was his reply. "Well, why do you have it priced so high?" He asked. "Because," replied the devil, "It is more useful to me than any of the others. I can pry open and get inside a man's consciousness with that one when I could not get near him with any of the others, and when once inside, I can use him in whatever way suits me best. It is so much worn because I use it with nearly everybody, as very few people yet know it belongs to me."

It hardly needs to be added that the devil's price for discouragement was so high that it was never sold. He still owns it and is still using it today.

> *"Having disarmed principalities and powers, He made a public spectacle of them, triumphing over them in it."* (Colossians 2:15)

Don't Fall For satan's Lies

Your arch-enemy, satan, has to deceive you into thinking that your Heavenly Father is against you, that He is angry with you because you have in some way failed Him. He tries to deceive you into thinking that your sickness or poverty Is The Father's Punishment for your sins.

I encourage you, do not fall for satan's lies. Never forget that satan is your arch-enemy. If Father has justified you, no one can bring a charge against you! It is impossible for satan to go before The Holy

Throne of God to accuse you. Instead, you have free access to God's Throne of Grace,

> *"Let us therefore come boldly to the throne of grace, that we may obtain mercy and find grace to help in time of need."* (Hebrews 4:16)

The Holy Blood of Jesus Christ, your Lord, has given you His Perfect Standing in The Presence of God. And, as a result, you no longer have to live with anger or disagreement with anyone when you wear God's Breastplate of Righteousness and keep your eyes and thoughts on Jesus.

> *"You will keep him in **perfect peace**, Whose mind is stayed on You, Because he trusts in You."*
> (Isaiah 26:3 bolding mine)

THE LIVER

The liver is the heaviest of all organs. It is located on the right side of the abdominal cavity, just below the diaphragm. Symbolically, it is the "pantry" of the body.

Physically, the liver aids in the production of energy in the body. The liver discharges chemicals essential for the digestion of the food we eat. When you get hungry, the liver begins to function more than usual to take advantage of everything available. It also absorbs all the essential vitamins and helps produce cholesterol in your body. Functions of the liver also include the formation of bile, cleaning the bloodstream, detoxification, and keeping off disease-causing pathogens.

Spiritually, the liver is symbolic of a deep fear of lacking the necessary essentials and believed to be required for living. Such as food, money, family, affection, love, etc. This deep fear can also cause a conflict within a person, wondering, *"What if I am not able to feed or provide for those of whom I feel responsible?"*

> *"Mine eyes do fail with tears, my bowels are troubled, my liver is poured upon the earth, for the destruction of the daughter of my people; because the children and the sucklings swoon in the streets of the city.* 12) *They say to their mothers, Where is corn and wine? ...."*
> (Lamentations. 2:11 & 12 KJV)

> *"He who did not spare His own Son, but delivered Him up for us all, how shall He not with Him also freely give us all things?"* (Romans 8:2)

Some Christians mistakenly believe that God Gives and also takes away. At funerals, we sometimes hear the minister say, *"The Lord giveth, and the Lord taketh. Blessed be The Name of The Lord."*

I remember when I was acquainted with a woman who suffered from brain cancer. I heard a Christian comment, *"You can't be sure what God's Will is. He may or may not heal."* That person meant that although The Lord had given this young woman life, He might later take her life away from her.

Job had the same attitude when he received the news that he had lost his property and children. Wrongly thinking that God was The Source of his problems and not knowing that it was actually satan who had come against him, he said,

> *"Naked I came from my mother's womb, and naked shall I return there. The Lord gave, and the Lord has taken away; blessed be the name of the Lord."* (Job 1:21)

Such a statement seems to honor God, but in reality, it reveals an inaccurate view of our Heavenly Father.

As Christians, we know that God is a Giver, not a taker! Jesus came to give us life more abundant. Jesus said that our arch-enemy, satan, is the thief. He comes to steal, kill, and destroy.

> *"The thief does not come except to steal, and to kill, and to destroy. I have come that they may have life, and that they may have it more abundantly."* (John 10:10)

The Scriptures reveal that Jesus met every need and healed every sickness brought before Him. **NEVER ONCE** did He take anything away from the people who came to Him. On The Cross at Calvary, He gave His life for us and said….

> *"So when Jesus had received the sour wine, He said, "**It is finished**!" And bowing His head, He gave up His spirit."* (John 19:30 bolding and underlining mine)

Jesus did **NOT** say, "It is finished all but for __________." The Desire of your Heavenly Father is for you to know today that He is The One Who Gives you all good things. And if He has already given us Heaven's Best — Jesus Christ, His Son, *"… how shall He not with Him also freely give us all things?"*

> *"He who did not spare His own Son, but delivered Him up for us all, how shall He not with Him also freely give us all things?"* (Romans 8:32)

> *"And my God shall supply all your need according to His riches in glory by Christ Jesus."* (Philippians 4:19)

EXCESSES CONTRIBUTE TO SERIOUS PROBLEMS

Excesses such as food, alcohol, drugs, excessive craving for greatness, aspirations, hopes, beliefs, etc., will contribute to severe problems. Sometimes our desire for excess is because we have difficulties knowing what is beneficial and harmful.

"Do not overwork to be rich; Because of your own understanding, cease! 5) Will you set your eyes on that which is not? For riches certainly make themselves wings; They fly away like an eagle toward heaven." (Proverbs 23:4 & 5)

Because our lives and fortunes are uncertain, we need to be conscientious of what we do with our lives.

"For riches are not forever, Nor does a crown endure to all generations." (Proverbs 27:24)

"For the drunkard and the glutton will come to poverty, And drowsiness will clothe a man with rags." (Proverbs 23:21)

"For where your treasure is, there your heart will be also." (Luke 12:34)

Your liver is symbolic of your withstanding everyday situations.

THE IMAGE YOU HAVE OF YOURSELF

In addition, the liver is symbolic of the image you have of yourself — the opinions you have of yourself. Due to our views, it is often difficult to accept the love of others or even our own affections towards others. Know who God says you are and believe and walk in it. You are....

Loved (John 3:16)

Dwelling In His Peace (Isaiah 26:3)

Lead In The Paths Of Righteousness (Psalms 23:3)

Walking Where He Leads Me (Psalms 37:23)

Casting Down Vain Imaginations (2 Corinthians 10:4-5)

Saved By Grace Through Faith (Ephesians 2:8-9)

Partaker Of His Divine Nature (2 Peter 1:4)

Delivered From The Power Of Darkness (Colossians 1:13)

A New Creature In Christ (2 Corinthians 5:17)

More Than A Conqueror (Romans 8:37)

Heir To The Blessings Of Abraham (Galatians 3:13-14)

Not Moved By What You See (2 Corinthians 4:18)

Healed By His Stripes (1 Peter 2:24)

Exercising Your Authority Over The Enemy (Luke 10:19)

An Heir Of Eternal Life (1 John 5:11-12)

Daily Overcoming The Devil (Deuteronomy 28:6)

Establishing God's Word Here On Earth (Matthew 16:19)

Above Only And Not Beneath (Deuteronomy 28:13)

The Light Of The World (Matthew 5:14)

Forgiven (Colossians 1:13-14)

Casting All Your Cares On Jesus (1 Peter 5:7)

Protected By God (Job 1:10)

Bringing Every Thought Into Captivity (2 Corinthians 10:5)

Kept In Safety Wherever You Go (Psalms 91:11)

Getting All Your Needs Met By Jesus (Philippians 4:19)

Justified (Romans 5:1)

Redeemed From The Curse Of The Law   (Galatians 3:13)

A Child Of God (Romans 8:16-17)

Led By The Spirit Of God (Romans 8:14)

Redeemed From The Hand Of The Enemy   (Psalms 107:2)

The Apple Of His Eye (Zechariah 2:8)

LEARN TO TRUST GOD FOR ALL YOUR NEEDS

"Behold, God is my salvation, I will trust and not be afraid; 'For YAH, the LORD, is my strength and song; He also has become my salvation.'" (Isaiah 12:2)

Always remember to:
- Keep your head high
- Keep your chin up
- Keep your shoulders back
- Keep your back straight and
- Keep your eyes on Jesus! He Desires to Bless you with His Grace and Unmerited Favor every day of your life.

"In righteousness you shall be established; you shall be far from oppression, for you shall not fear; and from terror, for it shall not come near you." (Isaiah 54:14)

GOD'S RIGHTEOUSNESS

Righteousness from the Strong's Concordance is defined as; upright virtuous, keeping the commands of God; innocent; faultless; guiltless; approved of or acceptable to God; integrity; virtue; purity of life, the correctness of thinking, feeling, and acting, in a narrower sense, rendering to each his due, in a judicial sense, passing just judgment of others, whether expressed in words or shown by the manner of dealing with them. In a broader sense, the state of him who he ought to be is righteousness, the condition acceptable to God. The person who trusts in Christ becomes *"the righteousness of God in Him."*

> *"For He made Him who knew no sin to be sin for us, that we might become the righteousness of God in Him."* (2 Corinthians 5:21)

You become in Christ Jesus all that God requires you to be, all that you could never be in yourself. Let's look at Abraham as an example. Abraham accepted The Word of God, making it his own — by that act of his mind and spirit which is called faith, and, as the sequel showed by submitting himself to God's Control. Therefore, God accepted him as one who fulfilled His Requirements.

> *"What does the Scripture say? Abraham believed God, and it was accounted to him for righteousness."* (Romans 4:3)

Abraham's faith in God did not mean instead of, but with a view to. He totally trusted God. This kind of faith thus exercised will bring your soul into vital union with God in Christ and inevitably produce righteousness of life. That is conformity to The Will of God.

> *"By the word of truth, by the power of God, by the armor of righteousness on the right hand and on the left."* (2 Corinthians 6:7)

> *"For He put on righteousness as a breastplate...."* (Isaiah 59:17a)

When God's Breastplate of Righteousness is firmly in place, it does not matter how many arrows your arch-enemy, satan, shoots at you. Not one of them will be able to penetrate.

Unfortunately, satan has persecuted and victimized so many in the Body of Christ that they are:

- Beaten down
- Trampled down
- Walking with their heads hung
- Shoulders slumped
- Eyes downcast

When your eyes are downcast, you cannot see Jesus. You are unaware of your righteousness. You cannot live or pray with confidence. You are convinced God can never Love you or benefit His Kingdom through you.

Your mentality, thoughts, feelings, and attitudes have everything to do with how well you perform in the midst of a battle. If you think you are defeated — you are defeated. However, as you develop an attitude of *"righteousness"* in your life and learn to view it through Jesus and His Sacrifice on The Cross at Calvary, your attitude will receive a Divine Impartation of God's Confidence and Boldness. Understanding this will **ALWAYS** put you on the winning side in His Victory.

> *"I will greatly rejoice in the LORD, My soul shall be joyful in my God; for He hath clothed me with the garments of salvation, He has covered me with the **robe of righteousness**, As a bridegroom decks himself with ornaments, And as a bride adorns herself with her jewels."* (Isaiah 61:10 bolding mine)

A robe covers from head to toe.

> *"Listen to Me, you who know righteousness, You people in whose heart is My law: Do not fear the reproach of men, Nor be afraid of their insults. 8) For the moth will eat them up like a garment, And the worm will eat them like wool; But My righteousness will be forever, And My salvation from generation to generation."* (Isaiah 51:7 & 8)

When dressed in God's Righteousness, wearing His Breastplate of Righteousness, we do not have to fear man or satan. God's Righteousness will sustain and keep us forever. It is eternal and stable. It lasts from generation to generation.

> *"For the arms of the wicked shall be broken, But the LORD upholds the righteous."* (Psalms 37:17)

God's Righteousness is
a lifestyle that produces
Victory in every situation

THE

GOSPEL

OF

PEACE

THE GOSPEL OF PEACE

"And your feet shod with the preparation of the gospel of peace." (Ephesians 6:15)

The shoes that the Roman soldier wore were made out of bronze or brass, usually brass, and were made of two parts: The greave and the shoe itself. The greave was a piece of metal that began at the top of the knee and extended down to rest on the upper part of the foot. They were made of a tube-like piece of metal, formed to fit around the calf of the Roman soldier, causing the shoes to look like boots made of brass. As were the other pieces of God's Armor, the greave was also beautifully engraved.

The shoe was made of two pieces of metal, one on the top of the foot and one on the bottom of the foot. The foot was covered with fine pieces of brass held together on the side by several pieces of sturdy leather. On the bottoms of their shoes were spikes anywhere from one inch to three inches long.

As the Roman soldiers marched down the cobblestone or marble-paved streets, imagine the sound they would make — the stomping of their shoes upon the pavement as they marched. This stomping of the boots served as a warning to the community. The soldiers were very egotistical and arrogant, and they stopped for no one. If anyone fell on the ground in their path, it was too bad. The Roman soldier just kept marching, stomping their wicked spikes on the pavement. Imagine what the person who fell in their pathway would look like after a whole group of men wearing shoes with spikes on the bottom of them had stomped over that person. How could Paul use the illustration of these killer shoes to describe peace?

Peace is both a defensive and offensive weapon. God's Peace not only protects us, but His Peace also, when used properly, keeps satan where he belongs — under our feet.

"And the God of peace shall bruise Satan under your feet shortly. The grace of our Lord Jesus Christ be with you. Amen." (Romans 16:20)

FEET from Strong's Concordance are described as; to make one a footstool of one's feet, i.e., to subject, to reduce under one's power; metaphor, taken from the practice of conquerors who placed their feet on the necks of their conquered enemies; of disciples listening to their teacher's instruction are said to be at his feet.

FEET from Vines is described as; besides its literal meaning, is used by metonymy [use of the name of one thing for that of another which it naturally suggests. Example: The pen (power of literature) is mightier than the sword (force).] A person in motion expresses subjection, what the foot can stand on.

SHOD from Strong's Concordance is described as; to under bind; to bind under one's self; bind on

PREPARATION from Strong's Concordance is described as; to make ready; prepare

PREPARATION from Vines denotes readiness; it also has the meaning of firm footing (foundation); the Gospel itself is to be the firm footing of the believer, his walk being worthy of it and therefore a testimony in regard to it. Those things, which God ordains.

Christianity is the tranquil state of a soul assured of its salvation through Christ, fearing nothing from God and content with its earthly lot of whatever sort that is.

Paul is saying God's Peace in our lives is foundational, the part on which the other parts rest or support. We have a firm footing when we have God's Peace.

God's Peace gives us a firm and sure foundation. His Peace will allow us to look at any challenge satan might bring our way and not be moved by what we see or hear. As a result, we are safe, protected, and sheltered. We can move out in confident faith without being moved by what we see or hear.

> *"Thou wilt keep him in perfect peace, whose mind*
> *is stayed on thee: because he trusteth in thee."*
> (Isaiah 26:3)

PEACE from Strong's Concordance is described as; a state of national tranquility, peace between individuals, security, safety, prosperity, fortune (because peace and harmony make and keep things safe and prosperous, Messiah's Peace).

PEACE from Vines is described as; harmonious relationships between men and God, friendliness, freedom from molestation, order, the sense of rest, and contentment.

There are two different kinds of peace:
- Peace **with** God
- Peace **of** God

When we accept Jesus Christ as our Lord and Savior, we receive **Peace with God**.

> *"And, having made peace through the blood of his cross, by him to reconcile all things unto himself; by him, I say, whether they be things in earth, or things in heaven."* (Colossians 1:20)

> *"And God purposed that through (by the service, the intervention of) Him <the Son> all things should be completely reconciled back to Himself, whether on earth or in heaven, as through Him, <the Father> made peace by means of the blood of His cross."* (Colossians 1:20 AMP)

It is possible to have **Peace with God** without experiencing The **Peace of God**. Many people are at Peace with God by virtue of their Salvation experience. However, they are not walking in The Peace of God. Instead of being liberated by His Established, Victorious Peace that passes all understanding, they walk in constant fretfulness, apprehension, concern, fear, anxiety, nervousness, worry, and all kinds of turmoil. As a result, we see God's people suffering from ulcers, sleeplessness, stress, physical sicknesses of all kinds, emotional turmoil, mental turmoil, chaos, confusion, uncertainty, misunderstanding, and more.

The **Peace of God** is a Protective Peace. It Protects us from fretfulness, apprehension, concern, fear, anxiety, nervousness, worry, and everything else satan would try to use to disrupt our enjoyment of God's Abundant Life.

"And let the peace of God rule in your hearts, to the which also ye are called in one body; and be ye thankful." (Colossians 3:15)

God has given us His Peace to hold us in place. When His Peace is firmly fixed in our mind, will, and emotions, there is nothing satan can do to move us. As we allow The **Peace of God** to rule our hearts and make all the decisions in our lives instead of fretfulness, apprehension, concern, fear, anxiety, nervousness, worry, and everything else satan would try to use, we will be overcoming conquers.

"And the peace of God, which passeth all understanding, shall keep your hearts and minds through Christ Jesus." (Philippians 4:7)

GOSPEL from Strong's Concordance is defined as; to bring good news, to announce glad tidings of the coming Kingdom of God, and The Salvation to be obtained in it through Jesus Christ, and of what relates to this Salvation.

HOW TO BE KEPT IN PERFECT PEACE

"You will keep him in perfect peace, whose mind is stayed on You, because he trusts in You." (Isaiah 26:3)

You need The Truth of God's Word to uproot any wrong beliefs you may have. I cannot express how important it is to get into His Holy Word and take time to meditate upon verses that reveal God's

Unwavering, Unfailing, Unconditional Love for you. That is what it takes to have your feet shod with the preparation of God's Peace.

For example, if you find your mind drifting into anxious thoughts over minor things, I encourage you to memorize and quote this Scripture verse:

> *"You will keep him in perfect peace, whose mind is stayed on You, because he trusts in You."* (Isaiah 26:3)

Whenever you feel stressed or worried about something, pull away from life's hustle and bustle and meditate on God's Promises. If possible, drive to a quiet park, or go somewhere where you can be alone with God for a time. Play some Anointed Worship music in your car or sing Worship to your God. The important thing is to focus on Him to quiet your mind and thoughts without interruption. Then feed on and speak aloud His Word, allowing it to permeate your spirit: *"God's Word declares, 'You will keep me in perfect peace, as my mind is stayed on You.'"*

Tell The Lord, *"Yes, Lord, it is You who will keep me in Your Perfect Peace. Perfect Peace comes only from You. I need to rest in Your Grace and keep my mind on You. I don't need to think about what to do about this challenge. You already have a Plan. As I trust in You and keep my mind stayed on You, You will Lead me and Guide me. My trust is not in my own strength, but in You and You alone, Jesus."*

Instead of allowing stress and worry to get to you, you are shodding your feet with the preparation of God's Peace and training your heart to see how God sees your challenges. The Bigger God becomes in your heart, the smaller your challenges become.

Many times, when I relax and keep my mind on The Lord, His Peace and Wisdom begin to flow in me, and the challenge that I was previously so apprehensive about becomes minute and inconsequential in The Presence of Almighty God.

If you are faced with what you feel is an impossible circumstance, learn to see what God Sees by meditating on His Word and letting His Peace drive out any anxiety. Allow His Peace and Wisdom to direct your paths.

THE HOLY SPIRIT LEADS US THROUGH PEACE

*"Then the dove came to him **in the evening**, and behold, a freshly plucked olive leaf was in her mouth; and Noah knew that the waters had receded from the earth."* (Genesis 8:11 bolding mine)

The Hebrew word for "time" is *eth*, which first appeared in the phrase *"in the evening"* in The Scripture passage above, we see that the first mention of right timing has to do with the dove — the dove is symbolic of The Holy Spirit. It's The Holy Spirit Who can Guide you to be at the right place at the right time.

The dove has an olive leaf in its mouth. When the flood during Noah's time ended, God sent a message through the dove bearing a leaf that there would be no more such worldwide flooding and destruction.

"And I will remember My covenant which is between Me and you and every living creature of

all flesh; the waters shall never again become a flood to destroy all flesh." (Genesis 9:15)

It was a message of God's Peace to men. It tells us that The Message The Holy Spirit brings is One of God's Peace.

The Holy Spirit leads you on the wavelength of God's Peace. Sometimes, when you are about to do something, perhaps sign a contract, make an agreement with someone, plan a vacation, or take part in some activity, you might feel an uneasiness, a lack of God's Peace. If that happens, **STOP** and take time to pray about what you are about to do because The Holy Spirit speaks to God's people through God's Peace or the lack of His Peace. He never speaks to us through nagging or accusations. He **ALWAYS LEADS** us through God's Peace. When your feet are not shod with God's Peace so that you are walking in God's Peace, then God's Peace is not in your heart, and it's time for you to reevaluate your decision and listen to His Leading. *There's another beautiful truth hidden in the first occurrence of the word **eth**. **Eth** appears in the phrase "in the evening" not only in Genesis 8:11 but also in other portions of Scripture.*

> *"And he made his camels kneel down outside the city by a well of water at **evening time**, the time when women go out to draw water."* (Genesis 24:11 bolding mine)

> *"So it was at the time of the going down of the sun that Joshua commanded, and they took them down from the trees, cast them into the cave where they had been hidden, and laid large stones*

against the cave's mouth, which remain until this very day." (Joshua 10:27 bolding mine)

When you study this out, you find that *evening time* is the time of our Lord, Jesus Christ's Finished Work on The Cross at Calvary.

The Old Testament priests had two daily sacrifices, one at 9 a.m. and the other at 3 p.m. Jesus was crucified at 9 a.m., and He died at 3 p.m., thus fulfilling the type of both the morning and evening sacrifices. At the time of *the evening* sacrifice, all of God's Judgment had fallen on the body of Jesus. The floods of God's Judgment were ended by The Sacrifice of Jesus Christ, our Lord, on The Cross at Calvary.

The Holy Spirit comes to you speaking God's Peace, telling you that there is now no enmity between you and God because His Judgment has passed. You are not perfect, but you can have and walk-in **Peace with God**. You can ask Him for His Success and be confident of His Covering in all that you do because all your sins have been judged in the body of His Beloved Son, Jesus Christ!

THE PEACE OF GOD
SETS YOU UP FOR SUCCESS

"There is no fear in love; but perfect love casts out fear, because fear involves torment. But he who fears has not been made perfect in love." (John 4:18)

God gives you His Peace to set you up for success in life. You cannot succeed in your marriage, family, and career when you are crippled and/or paralyzed with fear. Jesus Desires to do a work in your heart to liberate you from all your worries, whatever they may be. It may be the fear of failure, the fear of success, the fear of people's opinions of you, or even the fear that God is not with you.

All the fears that you experience in your life began with an untruth, a lie that you have somehow believed. Perhaps you have thought that God is angry and displeased with you and His Presence is far from you. That's why The Bible says,

> *There is no fear in love; but perfect love casts out fear, because fear involves torment. But he who fears has not been made perfect in love."* (John 4:18)

This Scripture tells us that when you begin to have a Revelation that God Perfectly Loves you (not because of what you have accomplished, but because of what Jesus has accomplished on The Cross at Calvary for you), that Revelation of The Unmerited Favor of God will cast out every fear, every lie, every anxiety, every doubt, and every worry that God is against you. The more you have a revelation of The Price Jesus Christ paid for you on The Cross at Calvary and how He has made you perfect, the more you will be able to free yourself to receive His Complete Peace and succeed in life!

As a believer in Jesus Christ, know that you have Absolute Peace with God. The New Covenant of Grace is also known as The Covenant of Peace. Today, as God's Child, you stand upon The Righteousness of Jesus and not your own righteousness. Today, because of Jesus, God says this to you….

> *"... I would not be angry with you, nor rebuke you.* 10) *For the mountains shall depart and the hills be removed, but My kindness shall not depart*

*from you, nor shall My **covenant of peace** be removed...."* (Isaiah. 54:9b & 10 bolding mine)

God is on your side. He Desires for your feet to be shod with His Preparation of The Gospel of Peace so that His Peace can help make you a success in life. All of Heaven's Resources are on your side, even if you are caught in the midst of a storm right now. Imagine eagle chicks sleeping soundly despite the storm, nestled under the wings of their mother, their protector, and provider. And may God's Peace which surpasses all understanding, guard your heart and mind through Christ Jesus.

> *"And the peace of God, which surpasses all understanding, will guard your hearts and minds through Christ Jesus."* (Philippians 4:7)

Shod your feet with the preparation of the gospel of peace, live in God's Peace, and rest in His Peace!

HOW TO BE LED BY PEACE

> *"Now may the Lord of peace Himself give you peace always in every way. The Lord be with you all."* (2 Thessalonians 3:16)

When you shod your feet with the preparation of the gospel of peace and God becomes Jehovah Shalom, the God of Peace, in your life, He doesn't just soothe your emotions. He will **Lead you with His Peace**.

For example, you may be making some decisions at your work, for your children, or perhaps even where and when to travel for your vacation. Talk to God about it. He will Lead and Guide you with His Peace. If there is Peace from The Lord, go with that decision. If His Peace is absent and you feel a sense of restraint, back away from it.

You will find that Guidance from The Lord comes very easily when God Manifests Himself as **JEHOVAH SHALOM**, The God of Peace. Decisions don't feel forced and/or full of strife. In His Peace, there is a Rest. His Peace will Guide you Supernaturally to be at the right place, at the right time, with the right people.

In Judges 6, the Midianites terrorized Israel day and night, destroying their crops and pillaging their livestock. The Lord assured Gideon, who was hiding from the Midianites, that He was with him and called Gideon a man of valor, a man of courage.

> *"... The LORD is with you, you mighty man of valor!"* (Judges 6:12b)

To which Gideon's response was,

> *"...O my lord, if the LORD is with us, why then has all this happened to us? And where are all His miracles which our fathers told us about, saying, 'Did not the LORD bring us up from Egypt?' But now the LORD has forsaken us and delivered us into the hands of the Midianites."* (Judges 6:13)

Gideon reminds us of ourselves. Instead of hearing that The Lord had just called him a man of valor, a man of courage, he began to complain. *"But now the LORD has forsaken us...."* Astoundingly, The LORD turned to him and said,

> *"Go in this might of yours, and you shall save Israel from the hand of the Midianites. Have I not sent you?"* (Judges 6:14)

What? First, The LORD calls this man who is in hiding *"a man of valor."* Now, He tells this complaining man, who is mad at God, to *"Go in this might of yours, and you shall save Israel...."*? Shouldn't God be saying something like, *"Be gone from My Presence, you stinking complainer, I must have found the wrong guy"*???

I am so thankful that The Lord is not like you and I are. He **ALWAYS** calls the things that are not as though they are.

> *"... God, who gives life to the dead and calls those things which do not exist as though they did"*
> (Romans 4:17b)

As you shod your feet with the preparation of the gospel of peace, you will receive a revelation of how The Lord is The God of Peace in your life. You may be fearful and complaining now, but God will send you to be a testimony of His Protection like He did Gideon. He will send you to your friends, coworkers, and loved ones who are bound by fear, and He will Anoint you to deliver them from fear!

Know That You Can Walk

In His Peace

Every day of Your Life

THE

SHIELD

OF

FAITH

THE SHIELD OF FAITH

"Above all, taking the shield of faith, wherewith ye shall be able to quench all the fiery darts of the wicked." (Ephesians 6:16)

*T*he shield of faith*"* is the only piece of God's Armor that tells you what will happen when you have it on and when you use it.

"Above all" means it is essential that *"the shield of faith"* surpasses all the other pieces of God's Armor. It is imperative that *"taking the shield of faith"* be first and foremost in our lives.

"... taking the shield of faith...." A shield is held up by one's arm and is supported by one's hand. The arm signifies force or strength. The hand represents power and direction.

SHIELD from the Strong's Concordance is described as; a door, an open door is used for the opportunity of doing something, the door of The Kingdom of Heaven (likened to a palace) denotes the conditions which must be complied with in order to be received into The Kingdom of God

SHIELD from Vines is described as; formerly meant a stone for closing the entrance of a cave; then, a shield large and oblong, protecting every part of the soldier; the work is used metaphorically of faith, which the believer is to take up in all as affecting the whole of his activities.

THE SHIELDS OF THE ROMAN SOLDIER

The Roman soldier owned two different shields. One was used in public displays such as parades and ceremonies, and the other shield was used in battle.

The soldier's shield used in parades and ceremonies was too small in size to carry into battle for their protection. This shield was for show and was often described as beautiful and magnificent. This shield was usually decorated with all kinds of etchings and engravings on the front. The middle portion of this shield often illustrated the artist's interpretation of previous victorious battles.

Sadly, there are Christians that only have a shield of faith that they use for display or parading around by telling others how much faith they have and talking about previous battles they have been a part of. But in reality, they do not have, nor do they know how to use God's Shield of Faith. They offer a lot of lip service for show without knowing how to use God's Shield of Faith in their lives or how to enter into battle with their arch-enemy, satan, and overcome him. With the battle shield, you are always prepared for the attacks of *"the wicked one."* But, when you fail to spend time with The Lord, you walk around with a parade shield, which displays the remembrance of the last battles won. It's beautiful, as you remember The Love, Strength, Power, and Magnificence of God that brought you through the previous battles victorious. But the parade shield carries **NO AUTHORITY** for the battle you are currently facing or the battle that may be ahead of you. This also tells you **WHO** your faith is in. Are you leaning on and trusting in God? Do you recognize your dependence on Him? Or are you still self-reliant in areas of your life? The areas of self-reliance are right where *"the wicked one"* aims for.

The Shield Used In Battle

The shield that the Roman soldier went into battle with was the size of a door. Most of their shields were made of up to six layers of tanned leather woven together so tightly they were almost as strong as steel. The battle shield was extremely hardwearing, strong, and durable.

Each morning when the Roman soldier would get up, he would reach for his battle shield, take a vial of oil, saturate a piece of cloth, and begin to rub the oil into the leather portion of the shield to keep it soft and flexible. If the shield were not properly cared for, the leather would become rigid, stiff, and brittle resulting in a failure to protect the soldier during battle.

> *"... I have been anointed with fresh oil."* (Psalms 92:10b)

The word *"anointed"* has to do with rubbing or covering a person. Rubbing is done with the hands. So, when we go into The Presence of God for a Fresh Anointing, we are asking The Holy Spirit to place His hand upon us and rub into us, and cover us from head to toe, in every part of our lives, with His Presence. Our very lives depend upon the everyday Anointing of The Holy Spirit.

When we keep our lives softened by The Anointing of The Holy Spirit, we are kept soft and flexible to God's Will. If not, we will become hard-hearted, stiff-necked, and brittle.

Faith And The Word Of God

> *"So then faith cometh by hearing, and hearing by the word of God."* (Romans 10:17)

Faith and The Word of God are so intimately tied together that if there is no Word, there is no Faith. Where there is no Faith, it is because The Word of God is not present.

When The Word of God is not present and active in our lives, it is only a matter of time before our sense of God's Peace is threatened by the concerns, worries, and cares of this life.

> *"And the cares of this world, the deceitfulness of riches, and the desires for other things entering in choke the word, and it becomes unfruitful."* (Mark 4:19 bolding mine)

FAITH

FAITH from Strong's Concordance is defined as; persuade, to be persuaded, to suffer one's self to be persuaded; to be induced to believe, to trust, have confidence, be confident fidelity, faithfulness, the character of one who can be relied on.

FAITH from Vines is defined as; primarily firm persuasion, a conviction based upon hearing, a firm conviction, producing a full acknowledgment of God's Revelation of Truth.

> *"And for this cause God shall send them strong delusion, that they should believe a lie:* 12) *That they all might be damned who believed not the truth, but had pleasure in unrighteousness."* (2 Thessalonians 2:11 & 12)

"But as many as received him, to them gave he power to become the sons of God, even to them that believe on his name." (John 1:12)

CONDUCT INSPIRED BY SURRENDER

"For we walk by faith, not by sight." (2 Corinthians 5:7)

Prominence is given to personal surrender to The Lord and conduct inspired by surrender. For example, the object of Abraham's faith was not God's Promise (that was the occasion of its exercise); his faith rested on God Himself.

"(As it is written, I have made thee a father of many nations,) before him whom he believed, even God, who quickeneth the dead, and calleth those things which be not as though they were.

20) He staggered not at the promise of God through unbelief; but was strong in faith, giving glory to God; 21) And being fully persuaded that, what he had promised, he was able also to perform." (Romans 4:17, 20 & 21)

JESUS IS OUR SHIELD OF FAITH

There are many excellent translations of The Scriptures that we enjoy. I often use several different ones when studying a subject or doing a particular word study. However, I have found that often the translators of many translations have changed some minor words. These translators probably felt these changes would help make The Scripture easier for the reader to understand. However, sometimes, they cause us to misinterpret the Meaning or Truth that Father meant for us to learn. I will use the following translations to make my case. First is The King James Version (KJV) because it is the closest translation to the original Greek and Hebrew writings. The second is The New King James Version (NKJV). The third is the New International Version (NIV). And fourth, the New American Standard (NAS). Using these translations and comparing them to each other, you will see how important and significant these small changes can be and how they can affect your understanding of The Word. I encourage you to get out the translation or version of The Word that you use and compare it along with the KJV as well.

THE MEASURE OF FAITH

From birth, every individual is given *"**the** measure **of faith**"* it takes for us to believe that Jesus is The Son of God.

> *"For I say, through the grace given unto me, to every man that is among you, not to think of himself more highly than he ought to think; but to think soberly, according as God hath dealt to every man **the** measure **of faith**."* (Romans 12:3 KJV bolding mine)

> *"For I say, through the grace given to me, to everyone who is among you, not to think of*

128

*himself more highly than he ought to think, but to think soberly, as God has dealt to each one **a** measure **of faith**.”* (Romans 12:3 NKJV bolding mine)

*“For by the grace given me I say to every one of you: Do not think of yourself more highly than you ought, but rather think of yourself with sober judgment, in accordance with **the** measure **of faith** God has given you.”* (Romans 12:3 NIV bolding mine)

*“For through the grace given to me I say to every man among you not to think more highly of himself than he ought to think; but to think so as to have sound judgment, as God has allotted to each **a** measure **of faith**.”* (Romans 12:3 NAS bolding mine)

FROM FAITH TO FAITH

The more we learn about Jesus, the more His Righteousness is revealed to us, our faith will grow and mature.

*“For therein is the righteousness of God revealed from faith **to** faith: as it is written, the just shall live **by faith**.”* (Romans 1:17 KJV bolding mine)

*“For in it the righteousness of God is revealed from faith **to** faith; as it is written, “The just shall live **by faith**.”* (Romans 1:17 NKJV bolding mine)

*"For in the gospel a righteousness from God is revealed, a righteousness that is **by faith** from first to last, just as it is written: "The righteous will live **by faith**.*" (Romans 1:17 NIV bolding mine)

*"For in it the righteousness of God is revealed from faith **to** faith; as it is written, "BUT THE RIGHTEOUS man SHALL LIVE **BY FAITH**.*" (Romans 1:17 NAS bolding mine)

ONE FAITH

The word faith here means trust, obey and have confidence in. As we grow and mature in The Lord, our confidence and trust grow in Him.

*"One Lord, **one faith**, one baptism.*" (Ephesians 4:5 KJV bolding mine)

*"One Lord, **one faith**, one baptism.*" (Ephesians 4:5 NKJV bolding mine)

*"One Lord, **one faith**, one baptism.*" (Ephesians 4:5 NIV bolding mine)

*"One Lord, **one faith**, one baptism.*" (Ephesians 4:5 NAS bolding mine)

His Faith, Jesus Is Faith

*"Behold, his soul which is lifted up is not upright in him: but the just shall live by **his faith**."* (Habakkuk 2:4 KJV bolding mine)

*"Behold the proud, His soul is not upright in him; But the just shall live by **his faith**."* (Habakkuk 2:4 NKJV bolding mine)

*"See, he is puffed up; his desires are not upright— but the righteous will live by **his faith**."* (Habakkuk 2:4 NIV bolding mine)

*"Behold, as for the proud one, His soul is not right within him; But the righteous will live by **his faith**."* (Habakkuk 2:4 NAS bolding mine)

The Faith of Jesus Christ

Jesus Is **EVERYTHING**. Our Christian life is all about Jesus.

*"Knowing that a man is not justified by the works of the law, but by **the faith of Jesus Christ**, even we have believed in Jesus Christ, that we might be justified by **the faith of Christ**, and not by the works of the law: for by the works of the law shall no flesh be justified."* (Galatians 2:16 KJV bolding mine)

*"Knowing that a man is not justified by the works of the law but by faith **in** Jesus Christ, even we have believed in Christ Jesus, that we might be justified **by faith in Christ** and not by the works of the law; for by the works of the law no flesh shall be justified."* (Galatians 2:16 NKJV bolding mine)

*"Know that a man is not justified by observing the law, but by faith **in** Jesus Christ. So we, too, have put **our faith in Christ Jesus** that we may be justified by faith **in** Christ and not by observing the law, because by observing the law no-one will be justified."* (Galatians 2:16 NIV bolding mine)

*"Nevertheless knowing that a man is not justified by the works of the Law but through faith **in** Christ Jesus, even we have believed in Christ Jesus, that we may be justified **by faith in Christ**, and not by the works of the Law; since by the works of the Law shall no flesh be justified."*
(Galatians 2:16 NAS bolding mine)

BY THE FAITH OF THE SON OF GOD

The life we now live is by The Faith **of** Jesus Christ, our Lord, The Son of God.

*"I am crucified with Christ: nevertheless I live; yet not I, but Christ liveth in me: and the life which I now live in the flesh I live by **the faith of the***

Son of God, *who loved me, and gave himself for me."* (Galatians 2:20 KJV bolding mine)

*"I have been crucified with Christ; and it is no longer I who live, but Christ lives in me; and the life which I now live in the flesh I live **by faith in the Son of God**, who loved me, and delivered Himself up for me."* (Galatians 2:20 NKJV bolding mine)

*"I have been crucified with Christ and I no longer live, but Christ lives in me. The life I live in the body, I live **by faith in the Son of God**, who loved me and gave himself for me."* (Galatians 2:20 NIV bolding mine)

*"I have been crucified with Christ; and it is no longer I who live, but Christ lives in me; and the life which I now live in the flesh I live **by faith in the Son of God**, who loved me, and delivered Himself up for me."* (Galatians 2:20 NAS bolding mine)

BY THE FAITH OF JESUS NOT BY OUR FAITH

*"According to the eternal purpose which he purposed in Christ Jesus our Lord: 12) In whom we have boldness and access with confidence by **the faith of him**."* (Ephesians 3:11 & 12 KJV bolding mine)

*"According to the eternal purpose which He accomplished in Christ Jesus our Lord, 12) In whom we have boldness and access with confidence **through faith in Him**."* (Ephesians 3:11 & 12 NKJV bolding mine)

*"According to his eternal purpose which he accomplished in Christ Jesus our Lord. 12) In him and **through faith in Him** we may approach God with freedom and confidence."* (Ephesians 3:11 & 12 NIV bolding mine)

*"This was in accordance with the eternal purpose which He carried out in Christ Jesus our Lord, 12) In whom we have boldness and confident access **through faith in Him**."* (Ephesians 3:11 & 12 NAS bolding mime)

THE FAITH OF JESUS

In any area you have bondage, The **Faith of Jesus** can set you free.

"Therefore if the Son makes you free, you shall be free indeed." (John 8:36)

Let's look at how trusting The Faith of Jesus reveals God's Son in you. Paul said,

"But when it pleased God, who separated me from my mother's womb, and called me by his grace,

134

16) *To **reveal his Son in me**, that I might preach him among the heathen; immediately I conferred not with flesh and blood:"* (Galatians 1:15 & 16 KJV bolding mine)

When you pray and ask God to heal you or someone else, you can rest, trust, and be at peace, knowing Father Desires to Heal. Father's Answering your request is **NOT** dependent upon your faith, works, self-efforts, or performance to qualify for Father to grant your request. The healing or need you have requested depends on your taking God's shield of faith and trusting Jesus and **His** Finished Work on The Cross at Calvary — **NOT** on you or your performance.

It is not about your faith — It is **ALL** about **HIS FAITH!**

It is all about Jesus!!!

Faith Is JESUS!!

Taking Up The Shield of Faith

Is Trusting In Jesus

Jesus Will Do What We Ask of Him

When We Realize

and Trust and Have Confidence

In The Fact That

Jesus Is Our Shield of Faith!!

WHAT ARE FIERY DARTS?

"... wherewith ye shall be able to quench all the fiery darts of the wicked." (Ephesians 6:16)

"...able to quench...." means to extinguish; put an end to; do away with; destroy

"...all the fiery...." these are destructive; inflamed with anger; torment; disease; grief; lust; etc.

"...darts...." Some translations have interchanged the word arrows for darts. To help bring clarity and understanding, I will use both terminologies, *"The fiery darts"* and *"the fiery arrows."*

"...of the wicked." Our arch-enemy, satan, attempts to bring strife, struggles, frustrations, anger, oppression, stress, lies, accusations, intimidation, shame, sickness, poverty, etc., into our lives. Jesus said,

> *"The thief does not come except to steal, and to kill, and to destroy. I have come that they may have life, and that they may have it more abundantly."* (John 10:10)

"The thief," satan, our arch-enemy, does his best to cause pain, trouble, misfortune, condemnation, shame, guilt, catastrophe, danger, and so much more to rob us of The More Abundant Life Jesus came to Provide for us.

THE FIERY DARTS
or
FIERY ARROWS USED IN BATTLE

There were three types of arrows or fiery darts used in battle.

1. Plain arrows that were similar to the ones used today.
2. Arrows dipped in tar were then set on fire and shot into the air.
3. Arrows that were filled with combustible fluids burst into flames upon impact.

The combustible arrows were made of long slender pieces of cane, filled with explosive fluids, and then disguised to look like normal, unassumingly dangerous arrows. They were used to cause injury and harm upon an equipped or prepared place. If the army had prepared its position so that the enemy could not easily break into and destroy it, then the enemy would go back to his old ways of using these deadly arrows of fire.

Some of the ways our arch-enemy, satan, may use the fiery darts to attack our emotions might be through:

Anger	Resentment	Apathy
Rage	Jealousy	Mistrust
Anxiety	Fear	Hatred
Worry	Insecurity	Hopelessness

A broken heart is one of the most challenging emotions a person will ever have to deal with. When our arch-enemy, satan, speaks, he may try to shoot fiery darts into our minds with thoughts like:

- You are going under financially.
- You have cancer.

- You will never find a mate.
- Your marriage is going to fail.
- Your children will never succeed.
- You are of no value to anyone.
- You have ruined your life by making the wrong choices.
- God cannot and will not use you because of....

I encourage you to remember that our arch-enemy, satan, speaks only negative things.

Have you ever been in the middle of a prayer meeting when suddenly a perverse or evil thought enters your mind? Your arch-enemy, satan, puts such thoughts in your mind. Then, he steps back, looks at you, and knocks you on your head, saying, *"How can you call yourself a Christian and still think such thoughts?"* He is trying to place you under condemnation through the bad thoughts **he** plants.

It is satan's idea to place you under bondage over the bad thoughts. Then you feel you have to repent of every one of those thoughts and seek God's Forgiveness. However, that is not what God's Word urges us to do. You see, God Desires us to bring *"every thought into captivity to the obedience of Christ."*

> *"Casting down arguments and every high thing that exalts itself against the knowledge of God, bringing every thought into captivity to the obedience of Christ."* (2 Corinthians 10:5)

Whose obedience are we to focus on? Christ's Obedience — not our own obedience!

IS IT MY OBEDIENCE?
or
THE OBEDIENCE OF CHRIST?

What is *"the obedience of Christ"*? It is His Obedience on The Cross at Calvary, where….

> *"... by one Man's obedience many will be made righteous."* (Romans 5:19)

Jesus shed His Blood for us on The Cross at Calvary. This means that when our arch-enemy, satan, tries to condemn us because of the thoughts he planted in our minds in the first place, we are to focus our thoughts on *"the obedience of Christ"* on The Cross at Calvary.

"The wicked one" can only attack our minds when he gets us to focus on our obedience instead of *"the obedience of Christ."* His strategy is to get us to examine our obedience or the lack of it, to determine our standing before God. Just as our position as sinners is not based on what we do, but what the first Adam did, in the same way, we are forever righteous today. Not because of what we do, but because of what Jesus Christ, the last Adam, did on The Cross at Calvary.

> *"Thus it is written, The first man Adam became a living being (an individual personality); the last Adam (Christ) became a life-giving Spirit <restoring the dead to life>."* (1 Corinthians 15:45 AMP)

Therefore, the next time satan tries to condemn you, I encourage you to say something along this line, *"According to 2 Corinthians 5:21, I am The Righteousness of God in Christ Jesus, and I chose to believe God's Word concerning me whether I have good or bad thoughts. My righteousness has nothing to do with my obedience. It is 'the obedience of Christ on The Cross at Calvary that has made me righteous."*

> *"For He made Him who knew no sin to be sin for us, that we might become the righteousness of God in Him."* (2 Corinthians 5:21)

*Thank You, Jesus, **THAT** through You; I have experienced The Divine Exchange — my sins for Your Righteousness.* Then, go ahead and pray, knowing that you have access to God and His Favor and that He hears the prayers of the righteous,

> *"The Lord is far from the wicked, But He hears the prayer of the righteous."* (Proverbs 15:29)

Check this out!

> *"And being ready to **punish all disobedience** when your obedience is fulfilled."* (2 Corinthians 10:6 bolding mine)

We punish the disobedience of our arch-enemy, satan when we obey by,

<blockquote>"Casting down arguments and every high thing that exalts itself against the knowledge of God, bringing every thought into captivity to the obedience of Christ." (2 Corinthians 10:5)</blockquote>

How exciting!!! By obeying God's Word, His Holy Scriptures, we punish satan for what he **tried** to condemn us with.

Any thought that does not remind you of who you are in Christ Jesus — is a fiery dart.

Preparing For Battle

Just before the Roman soldier went into battle, he dipped his shield into a tub of water, causing the leather to become somewhat more flexible. When the fiery darts hit the wet shield, they would bounce off and be extinguished. This is symbolic of us opening our hearts and lives to our Lord, Jesus Christ, and allowing His Word to wash, cleanse, and purge us.

<blockquote>"That he might sanctify and cleanse it with the washing of water by the word." (Ephesians 5:26)</blockquote>

If we do not open our hearts and lives to Him and allow His Word to wash, cleanse, and purge us, we will become hardhearted, anxious, fretful, cracked in our beliefs, and broken by life's circumstances. This, too, places us in danger during battle.

THE PARADE SHIELD

When you fail to spend time with your Lord, you are walking around with your parade shield. As stated earlier, the parade shield displays etchings and inscriptions in remembrance of the last battles won. It may be beautiful, and as you look on it, you remember the Love, Strength, Power, Provision, and Magnificence of God that brought you through the last battles victorious. But the parade shield carries NO AUTHORITY for the current battle you are in or the battle you may be facing. This also tells you who your faith is in. Are you leaning on God? Do you recognize your dependence on Him? Or are you still self-reliant in areas of your life? The areas of self-reliance are right where satan, *"the wicked one,"* aims for with his *"fiery darts."*

YOU ARE VICTORIOUS

You are Victorious. You already have everything in Christ that you need.

> *"Therefore let no one boast in men. For all things are yours: 22) whether Paul or Apollos or Cephas, or the world or life or death, or things present or things to come — all are yours. 23) And you are Christ's, and Christ is God's."* (1 Corinthians 3:21 & 23)

You are blessed with every spiritual blessing in Christ,

"Blessed be the God and Father of our Lord Jesus Christ, who has blessed us with every spiritual blessing in the heavenly places in Christ."
(Ephesians 1:3)

"The wicked one," your arch-enemy, satan, knows this. That is why he sends his *"fiery darts"* to deceive you and make you think you don't have nor will you ever have God's Victory.

Over and over, satan attacks you by saying things like, *"Look at that small sum in your bank account! How are you going to pay the bills?"* Stand your ground. Put up God's Shield of Faith. Declare, *"I am not trying to be rich. I am already blessed in Christ!"* It doesn't matter how much you have in the bank. You are richly supplied because you are in Christ, and as the need arises, His Provision and Supply will be there **if** you believe it.

It is the same thing with healing. *"the wicked one,"* satan, will try to attack you with symptoms in your body. He will try to put pain in your body and make you feel weak, tired, and/or frail so that you think you are sick. His goal is to make you believe that you don't have God's Healing. That is the time to be conscious of The Finished Work of Jesus Christ on The Cross at Calvary. Jesus said,

"It is finished: and he bowed his head, and gave up his spirit." (John 19:30)

I encourage you to put out that fiery dart by picking up God's Shield of Faith and declaring, "I am not trying to get healed; I am healed! I am standing on The Victory Ground, which Jesus has given me!"

We Are Fighting From Victory
Not
Fighting For Victory

The Helmet of Salvation

The Helmet of Salvation

"And take the helmet of salvation...." (Ephesians 6:17a)

The Helmet that the Roman soldier wore was like all his other armor pieces (except the belt). His helmet was very striking and elaborate. It was more like a beautiful sculpture with all kinds of engravings and etchings than a helmet. Many helmets had pastoral farm scenes with all sorts of animals on them. Often the entire helmet was fashioned to look like the head of an elephant, the head of a horse, or some other animal.

The Roman soldiers' helmets were bronze and specially designed to protect their cheeks, jaws, and necks. On the very top of the soldier's helmets were massive plumes of brightly colored feathers or brightly colored horse hair that stood straight up out of it. If the helmet was to be worn in a parade or ceremony, the brightly colored plume could be long enough to hang to the soldier's back. It was so enormous and strong that nothing could penetrate it — not a hammer or battle-ax. Because the helmet was so large and heavy, it was lined with a sponge to soften its weight when on the soldier's head.

When you look at a person, you usually see their face or head first. As a Christian, our Salvation is the most Beautiful, Magnificent, Multifaceted, Involved, Complicated Gift God has ever given us.

SALVATION in The Strong's Concordance is defined as: deliverance, preservation, and safety, saved from the penalty, power, presence, and sin.

Salvation describes The Grace of God.

> *"For the grace of God that bringeth salvation hath appeared to all men."* (Titus 2:11)

When we are confident in our Salvation, we walk in **THE POWERFUL REALITY** of what Salivation means to us, and we are noticeable.

Some Christians may think, *"I'm saved through Jesus Christ. Therefore, I already have on God's Helmet of Salvation, so I've got the helmet part under control."* However, The Word tells us Salvation is not only about being saved from hell.

The main reason you wear God's Helmet of Salvation is to protect your mind and guard your thoughts.

> *"But let us who are of the day be sober, putting on the breastplate of faith and love, and as a helmet the hope of salvation."* (1 Thessalonians 5:8)

THE DIFFERENCE BETWEEN FAITH AND HOPE

Faith speaks of now. Faith is trusting and believing that right now, in Christ Jesus, you have the answer to your need even though you do not see it yet.

What is hope? Hope speaks of the future. Hope is a confident expectation of good to come. The Word states it this way, *"the blessed hope and glorious appearing"* of Jesus,

> *"Looking for the blessed hope and glorious appearing of our great God and Savior Jesus Christ."* (Titus 2:13)

In today's world, the word "hope" is used nonchalantly and thoughtlessly. We say things like, *"I hope that cake is chocolate"* or *"I don't know whether or not I will get it, but hope so, I am keeping my fingers crossed"* or *"I hope this or that doesn't happen"* or *"I hope so"* or *"I hope not"* you get what I am saying. This kind of hope means that you are not sure about something. But, again, "hope" in The Word means a positive or confident expectation of good. So, when God says, *"Have hope,"* He says you are to have a confident expectation that good things will happen to you.

You have no idea what will happen in your life this week. But it is God's Desire for you to put on His Helmet of Salvation, and in doing so, you will have a confident expectation that good will happen to you. You can know this in your heart. Declare aloud with your mouth that it will be a good week. Declare that you will see God's Preservation, His Wholeness, His Health, and His Prosperity in your life. This is the attitude you will have when wearing God's Helmet of Salvation.

Know in your knower that you will have a great week in The Name of Jesus! God did not say to you, "According to God's Will be it unto you." **No**, He said,

> *"... According to your faith and trust and reliance*
> <on the power invested in Me> *be it done to you."*
> (Matthew 9:29 AMP)

If a person says something like, *"This is going to be a horrible week, I just know it."* They are right. But the person that says, *"I know this is going to be a blessed week,"* is also right. Every individual will have the kind of week that they expect to have. I am not saying that every week will be a bed of roses if you expect good. I am saying that even if there is a storm, Jesus will give you His Peace, His Ideas, and His Strategies to deal with it. He said,

> *"I have told you these things, so that in Me you may have <perfect> peace and confidence. In the world you have tribulation and trials and distress and frustration; but be of good cheer <take courage; be confident, certain, undaunted>! For I have overcome the world. <I have deprived it of power to harm you and have conquered it for you.>"* (John 16:33 AMP)

I encourage you, expect a good week! Speak aloud that the coming week will be good because Jesus Christ, your Lord, has overcome this world, and you choose to trust in Him.! Hope is a confident expectation of good to come.

The world's kind of hope is not The Hope Jesus Christ offers to His people.

The helmet that the Roman soldier wore was so strong and fit so tightly around his head that the enemy could not penetrate his helmet when they came at him with a battle-ax or hammer. Without the helmet, the soldier could lose his head. If we do not have on God's Helmet of Salvation fitting tightly on our heads, when our arch-enemy, satan, comes at us with a hammer to attack our minds or his battle-ax to steal our victory, he will succeed.

Your arch-enemy, satan, will lie and try to chip away at your foundation, trying to tell you that Healing, Deliverance, Preservation, and Soundness of mind are not a part of Salvation through The Redemptive Work that Jesus Christ paid for on The Cross at Calvary. By the time satan is done with you, all he leaves you with is Heaven.

Sadly, numerous Christians are trying to **Do the work** of God without making a personal goal to walk in the full knowledge of their Salvation, and they are spiritually slaughtered.

> *"Put on the whole armor of God, that you may be able to stand against the wiles of the devil."*
> (Ephesians 6:11)

> *"Lest Satan should get an advantage of us: for we are not ignorant of his devices."* (2 Corinthians 2:11)

God's Helmet of Salvation protects our minds. Our arch-enemy, satan, comes at us through our minds. He tries to play "mind games" with us. He brings with purpose his:

♦ deception	♦ guilt
♦ dishonesty	♦ shame
♦ fraud	♦ condemnation
♦ accusation	♦ slander
♦ blame	♦ etc.

He baits us to perceive lies as truth or truth as lies, and if we bite into it, his trickery and deception will be fully implemented into our lives.

> *"For the weapons of our warfare are not carnal, but mighty through God to the pulling down of strong holds."* (2 Corinthians 10:4)

STRONGHOLDS

If we have strongholds in our lives, mentally and/or emotionally, we have walls around ourselves that are so thick that others, which could help us, cannot seem to break through that obstruction. These invisible walls keep people from getting through to us. These invisible walls or strongholds keep people from getting too close to us. Our arch-enemy, satan, would like to keep us isolated and removed from those who could help bring freedom to our lives.

TWO DIFFERENT CHARACTERISTICS OF STRONGHOLDS

RATIONAL AND IRRATIONAL:
- Rational fears and worries that make sense.
- Irrational fears and anxieties are entirely unrealistic.

> *"For God hath not given us the spirit of fear; but of power, and of love, and of a sound mind."* (2 Timothy 1:7)

Too many of God's people live in fear of:
- sickness
- disease
- dying
- rejection
- financial lack
- financial ruin
- etc.

These fears can place a person in prison. A prison of:

♦ Fearing rejection — keeps us from developing relationships in our lives.

♦ Fearing marriage — hinders us from functioning in the marital relationship as God intended.

♦ Fearing potential failure — keeps us from stepping out to do something.

♦ Etc.

All too often, we try to be logical about things, but logical thinking leads to an unsubmitted mind that tries to talk you out of obeying God. If the rational mind is not submitted to God, it will completely dominate and control one's obedience to God.

> *"Casting down imaginations, and every high thing that exalteth itself against the knowledge of God, and bringing into captivity every thought to the obedience of Christ."* (2 Corinthians 10:5)

Our arch-enemy, satan, often makes things appear so significant in our minds that we cannot share them with anyone else. Yet, they often lose their power almost instantly when we tell our spouse or friend what we have been battling and/or thinking about.

You must recognize where these thoughts are coming from and address them straightforwardly. If you do not take your thoughts captive, your thoughts will take you captive. The sole purpose of your arch-enemy, satan, is to manipulate and control you. As you put on God's Helmet of Salvation, you submit and listen to what God has to say through His Word and other godly men and women.

STRONGHOLD OF OPPRESSION

Oppression is a force that comes to powerfully dominate and manipulate your mind. Picture a tyrant who tries to forcibly impose their will upon someone. They may tell the person what to:

- eat
- wear
- think

Or how to:

- manage money
- plan for their future
- dress

Or they may tell them what their self-image is:

- You are ugly.
- You are stupid.
- You're hopeless.
- You will never amount to anything.

When a stronghold is unchallenged and oppression sets in, the end result is hopelessness.

> *"Wherefore gird up the loins of your mind, be sober, and hope to the end for the grace that is to be brought unto you at the revelation of Jesus Christ."* (1 Peter 1:13)

Through God's Helmet of Salvation, your knower knows that you have Salvation from:

- sins
- condemnation

- shame
- guilt
- doubt
- fear
- hell

You have:

- Protection
- Preservation
- Healing
- Soundness of mind
- Peace
- Joy
- Freedom
- Etc.

The only way your arch-enemy, satan, can successfully attack you is through your mind. You must recognize your responsibility to these strongholds. Recognize these strongholds are satan's way of trying to reinstate your mind into your old way of thinking before you met Jesus Christ and accepted Him as your Lord.

God intends your mind to think like the mind of Christ and be controlled by The Holy Spirit. You do this by reading and applying The Word of God to your life. I once heard a man of God say, *"If you want to act right, you must believe right."* You can achieve right thinking and right believing by applying God's Word to your life.

"But we have the mind of Christ." (1 Corinthians 2:16)

"Let this mind be in you, which was also in Christ Jesus." (Philippians 2:5)

It is through your mind that satan tries to control and manipulate your emotions. When you allow this, you are agreeing to open a door that will begin to permit satan, your arch-enemy, to send sickness and disease in your body and so on.

HOW DO WE RECEIVE THE MIND OF CHRIST?

Get in touch with The Power of God.

"Finally, my brethren, be strong in the Lord, and in the power of his might." (Ephesians 6:10)

THE POWER OF GOD COMES THROUGH

- His Word
- His Influence
- His Presence
- His Faith
- His Love
- His Peace
- His Knowledge
- His Wisdom
- His Discernment
- His Understanding
- His Grace
- His Strength
- Obedience to Him
- His Foreknowledge
- Etc.

When His Power and Strength come to you, it will clothe you with His Armor and make you complete.

TAKE THE HELMET OF SALVATION

"And take the helmet of salvation." (Ephesians 6:17a)

The word *"take"* is translated as "receive" forty times in The New Testament. Thus, the verse would be better translated, *"And receive the helmet of salvation."*

For your Protection, God has given you His Salvation as a Helmet. However, He will not force a renewed mind on you.

You put on God's Helmet of Salvation by studying and allowing God's Word, His Holy Scriptures, to transform your life, changing your conduct and experiences. I encourage you to become surrounded mentally and emotionally with God's Helmet of Salvation.

A STRONG PERSON
VS.
PERSON OF STRENGTH

A strong person works out every day to keep their body in shape.
A person of strength kneels in prayer to keep their soul in shape.

A strong person isn't afraid of anything.
A person of strength shows courage in the midst of their fear.

A strong person won't let anyone get the best of them.
A person of strength gives the best of themselves to everyone.

A strong person makes mistakes and avoids the same in the future.

A person of strength realizes life's mistakes can also be God's Blessings and capitalizes on them.

A strong person wears a look of confidence on their face.

A person of strength wears God's Grace.

A strong person walks sure-footed.

A person of strength knows God will catch them when they fall.

A strong person has faith that they are strong enough for the journey.

A person of strength has faith that it is in the journey that they will become strong.

Author Unknown

THE

SWORD

OF

THE

SPIRIT

THE SWORD OF THE SPIRIT

"... and the sword of the Spirit, which is the word of God." (Ephesians 6:17b)

The Roman soldiers used five different types of swords against their enemies.

1. The gladius sword was extremely heavy, broad-shouldered with an amazingly long blade. This one was the most stunning and useful of all the swords because of its weight. It was so enormous and heavy that it was referred to as a two-handed sword. The Roman soldier had to use both hands to wield it, as it had to be swung with all the soldier's might.

This sword was razor-sharp on one side and blunt and dull on the other. After suffering a disastrous defeat by the Carthaginians, the Romans discarded these large swords, developing other swords similar to the one the Carthaginians had used to defeat them.

2. This sword was shorter and narrower. It was about seventeen inches long and about two-and-one-half inches in width. Since this sword was much lighter, it was easier to carry and swing.

3. This sword was even shorter than the second one. It looked more like a dagger than a sword. It was carried in a small hidden case beneath the soldier's outer coat and was used to stab the enemy in the heart.

4. This sword was long and slender and was mainly used by the

cavalry. This sword is similar to those used in modern-day fencing. Not the kind of sword used in hand-to-hand combat in battle.

5. This is the type of sword Paul had in mind. This weapon of murder was approximately nineteen inches long and was razor-sharp on both sides of the blade. The very end of the sword turned upward, causing the point of the blade to be extremely sharp and deadly.

This two-edged sword inflicted a wound far worse than the other swords. After the Roman soldier penetrated his enemy's stomach, he held the sword with both hands, gave the sword a jerking twist, and withdrew the person's entrails as he pulled the sword from his enemy's body.

Of all the swords available, this was the most dangerous of all. **This one was a terror to the imagination. This sword is** intended to kill and completely rip an enemy's insides to shreds.

THE SWORD OF THE SPIRIT

God's Holy Scriptures, His Holy Word, is God's Sword of The Spirit. His Sword hangs from The Belt of Truth. This means you will not be able to apply God's Sword or His Word effectively unless you are wearing God's Belt of Truth to hang His Sword on. In other words, if you are not honest, have no integrity, if you are not upright and reliable, and the words you speak are not the truth, God's Sword, His Word, will not be effective in your life. If those around you cannot see you living what you speak, they will not trust what you say, neither will they believe you when you talk about Jesus or the things of God.

SWORD in The Strong's Concordance is defined as a large knife used for killing animals and cutting up flesh; a small sword, as distinguished from a large sword; a curved sword, for a cutting stroke; a straight sword, for thrusting.

SPIRIT in The Strong's Concordance is defined as; The Third Person of The Triune God. A Life-giving Spirit; to breath; and to blow. God, The Holy Spirit, is coequal, coeternal with God, The Father, and God His Son, Jesus Christ.

RHEMA WORD

When using God's Sword of The Spirit, we have to apply it with The Rhema Word of God.

REHEMA WORD in The Strong's Concordance is defined as; it is a matter of command; an utterance; a declaration of one's mind made into words; that which is or has been uttered by the living voice, thing spoken; any sound produced by the voice and having definite meaning; a matter of dispute, case at law.

A RHEMA WORD OF GOD IS:
- Spoken clearly.
- Spoken powerfully.
- Spoken in unmistakable terms.
- Spoken in undeniable language.
- Spoken in unquestionable, specific, confident, and definite terms.

A Rhema Word from The Lord that The Holy Spirit Supernaturally drops into your mind or heart causes The Word to come Alive and Impart God's Special Power into you. Your knower knows something, and no one can take that from you.

> *"The entrance of Your words gives light; It gives understanding to the simple."* (Psalms 119:30)

> *"But the Helper, the Holy Spirit, whom the Father will send in My name, He will teach you all things, and bring to your remembrance all things that I said to you."* (John 14:26)

In other words, The Holy Spirit will bring to your remembrance a specific word at a specific time, for a specific purpose, and faith and trust in God will fill your whole being.

This kind of word gives you *"sword"* power in the spirit realm. When this word comes up out of your spirit, it will reveal to you what to say and the way to go. This kind of word is The Holy Spirit's rejection of satan's attempts to penetrate and infiltrate your mind with malicious lies, deceptions, and accusations.

EXAMPLES OF RHEMA WORDS

- ◆ Noah — Genesis 6:13 - 7:4
- ◆ Abraham — Genesis 12:1-3
- ◆ Joseph — Genesis 37:6-9
- ◆ Moses — Exodus 3 & 4
- ◆ Mary, mother of Jesus — Luke 2:28-33, 35-37
- ◆ Paul — Acts 9:4-6
- ◆ Ananias — Acts 9:10-16

Rehema Words are specifically spoken, powerfully given, unmistakable, undeniable Words from God. They may be brief and straight to the point or long and expressive, but they **ALWAYS** do a great deal of Damage to the domain of darkness.

Jesus needed a Rhema Word:

> *"Then Jesus was led up by the Spirit into the wilderness to be tempted by the devil. 2) And when He had fasted forty days and forty nights, afterward He was hungry. 3) Now when the tempter came to Him, he said, 'If You are the Son of God, command that these stones become bread.'"* (Matthew 4:1-3)

Jesus faced His arch-enemy, satan, the same way we do every day of our lives.

> *"But He answered and said, "It is written...."*
> (Matthew 4:4a)

It is not enough to just know God's Word in your heart. You have to speak it aloud. You turn latent power into God's Actual Power by speaking God's Word aloud. Jesus in the wilderness did not think of Scripture or hum them in His head. He spoke The Scriptures out loud.

A person can memorize thousands of Scriptures, but if they don't speak aloud, *"It is written...."* They will **NOT** actually release The Word. Until The Word is released from your mouth, there will be no actual Power. Jesus is our example.

Because The Word was already stored up inside of Jesus, The Spirit of God could draw it out of Him to speak out loud, like a deadly blade. The spoken Rhema Word is what satan wishes you to overlook and neglect.

FOR EXAMPLE

Perhaps you are concerned about health, finances, family, politics, employment, relationships, or your future in general.

Sometimes, even when all seems well, some still worry because they have heard what others have said. Sadly, sometimes Christians say something like this to one another, *"You should worry when everything is peaceful because something is wrong when the devil leaves you alone."* Therefore, they worry even when there is nothing to worry about! All too often, living in peace of mind seems abnormal to many.

"Therefore I say to you, do not worry about your life, what you will eat or what you will drink; nor about your body, what you will put on. Is not life more than food and the body more than clothing?" (Matthew 6:25)

Jesus, our Lord, does not Desire for us to worry about anything. He tells us not to worry about our daily needs and provisions. Our Father knows what we need, and He Desires to add these things to us.

"For after all these things the Gentiles seek. For your heavenly Father knows that you need all these things. 33) But seek first the kingdom of God and His righteousness, and all these things shall be added to you. 34) Therefore do not worry about tomorrow, for tomorrow will worry about its own things. Sufficient for the day is its own trouble." (Matthew 6:32-34)

Our God is the same God who took care of the children of Israel in the wilderness. He fed them with angels' food, manna from Heaven every day for 40 years! (Exodus 16) Under His Care, His people had no lack. When the people craved meat for dinner, He simply rained quails on them.

"And the people stayed up all that day, all night, and all the next day, and gathered the quail (he who gathered least gathered ten homers); and they spread them out for themselves all around the camp." (Numbers 11: 32)

The children of Israel only had to pick them up. If they had gone out into the desert to look for meat themselves, they probably would not have found any.

The problem with us today is that we think we must **DO** something to help ourselves. Some of us may even think that it is easy for Jesus to say, *"Don't worry. Take no thought for your life"* because He does not understand the problems we face in life.

The Truth is, Jesus **DOES UNDERSTAND** the problems we face in life. In fact, He faced what I would call the final problem — death.

Death is the final problem because it puts an end to all our other problems. Jesus faced death on The Cross at Calvary. He Conquered death and Rose From The Dead. And because He Conquered The Problem of problems, we can trust Him when He tells us not to worry!

> *"So He humbled you, allowed you to hunger, and fed you with manna which you did not know nor did your fathers know, that He might make you know that man shall not live by bread alone; but man lives by **every word** that proceeds from the mouth of the Lord."* (Deuteronomy 8:3 bolding mine)

The Rehema Word of God fed the children of Israel for 40 yrs. and Empowered Jesus to resist temptation. The Power of The Sword of The Spirit hinges upon The Presence or Absence of God's Word in your life.

THE TWO-EDGED SWORD

> *"For the word of God is living and powerful, and sharper than any two-edged sword, piercing even to the division of soul and spirit, and of joints and marrow, and is a discerner of the thoughts and intents of the heart."* (Hebrews 4:12)

One side of the sword came into being when The Word of God was initially spoken from the mouth of God. The second edge is added when The Word of God is spoken out of our mouths.

This is only one reason why meditation on and the confession of The Word of God is vital in your life. When you allow The Word to come in, it will change you inwardly, causing a change that others can see outwardly. When God's Truth begins to take root in your soul, it releases God's Transforming Power in you, which will then release Spiritual Power from you.

"To the law and to the testimony! If they do not speak according to this word, it is because there is no light in them." (Isaiah 8:20)

Let Us Do As David Did
"Your Word have I hidden in my heart...." (Psalms 119:11)

THE

LANCE

OR

SPEAR

OF

PRAYER

THE LANCE OR SPEAR OF PRAYER

"Praying always with all prayer and supplication in the Spirit, being watchful to this end with all perseverance and supplication for all the saints — and for me, that utterance may be given to me, that I may open my mouth boldly to make known the mystery of the gospel." (Ephesians 6:18)

The Roman soldier used many different kinds of lances or spears. Most Roman soldiers carried short and long lances or spears, one long lance and five shorter ones. These lances or spears varied from six feet long to twenty-four feet long. Some had iron heads shaped like a leaf, others a sharp barb, and some a gagged point. The shorter lances or spears were used for gouging and thrusting an enemy up close, while the longer ones were used for hurling at an enemy from a distance. After successfully striking an enemy with his lance or spear, the Roman soldier would take his sword and decapitate him.

THE LANCE OR SPEAR OF PRAYER

For The Child of God, the various kinds of lances or spears are symbolic of the various types of prayer in their prayer life. Prayer is a Powerful Weapon that is thrust forward into the spirit realm against the malicious and wicked works of our arch-enemy, satan. Prayer is The Divine piece of God's Armor that has the Ability and Power to stop major barriers and/or obstacles developing in our lives.

PRAYING in The Strong's Concordance is defined as: to pray to God; to wish, to pray, to pray for.

PRAYER in The Strong's Concordance is defined as: prayer addressed to God: a place set apart or suited for the offering of prayer; expresses confiding access to God; the element of devotion; to that of childlike confidence; by representing prayer as the heart's conversion with God.

Prayer is simply communication with The Father. His heart Desires that a relationship develops between the two of you that you and He become the dearest and closest friends. You can come in prayer, talk with Him, inquire of Him, ask of Him, request things of Him, and consult with Him. Sometimes you may even intercede on behalf of someone else with Him. You can pray and communicate to Him all the matters that concern you as an individual and others. There is nothing in your life that does not concern Him — nothing that He does not Desire to be a part of. He is I Am.

Through talking to Him, you learn how to communicate with Him. A relationship between the two of you is formed, and you become one mind with Him.

"Can two walk together, unless they are agreed?" (Amos 3:3)

Based upon The Word of God, our prayer life requires us to come into agreement with God. Our prayers, our communication with Him, should always be centered around pleasing Him.

PRAYER IS A FORM OF WORSHIP

Prayer is a form of Worship, the outpouring of our hearts. Prayer is turning to The Father as our Source in our time of hardship, believing He Alone is The Deliverer and can Deliver us from all our problems. He Alone is The Provider and has Provision for our every necessity. He Alone is The Answer to our every question.

More than that, prayer is powerful communication with The Father. Our prayer life is where we truly learn how to build a relationship with Him and come into agreement with Father and walk with Him, please His heart, and live in His Trust and Peace.

PRAYING ALWAYS — it may sound complicated and even confusing to pray always. How can we pray at all times?

- One way is to make brief prayers as your consistent reaction to every circumstance that comes your way throughout the day.

- ♦ Another way is to enjoin your life around God's Desires and Teachings so that your entire life becomes a prayer.

You don't have to remove yourself from others or from your place of work to pray always. You can make prayer your life and your life a prayer.

SUPPLICATION in The Strong's Concordance is defined as; to want, lack; to desire, long for; to pray, make supplications; denotes a request of the will; the asking of the need; a seeking, asking, entreating, petition to God.

SUPPLICATION IN THE SPIRIT — Whenever you come to your Father in prayer, you need to come in humility and pray according to The Spirit's Leading or in tongues. When we pray out of our own will, we are not praying for The Will of God.

SOULISH PRAYERS

Soulish prayers are requests, petitions, or communications that come out of a person's mind, will, and/or emotions. Soulish prayers are prayed out of our flesh. Anytime anything is done out of our flesh, the motive is selfish.

Praying Out of
Our Own Understanding

The mind is intellect, thought, mentality, intuition, perception, conception, acceptance, ego, judgment, understanding, theory, reasoning, instinct, and/or subconscious thought.

Our minds are very complex. No two people think alike. We are so uniquely made and designed that we genuinely are individuals in every aspect of the word. Yet, every person must understand some basic foundational principles to communicate and function in society. We all require social skills, math skills, reading skills, occupational ability, etc. We are so different and yet, so alike.

This is also true when it comes to our reasonings, understandings, our perceptions, and our thought processes. We live in a society in which we often are forced into making judgment calls or snap decisions. As a result, we have become self-reliant. This, sadly, has carried over into our prayer lives.

Some time ago, I faced a challenging health issue. Having had three previous back surgeries, the Drs. told me in 2001 that a fourth back surgery would undoubtedly leave me paralyzed if attempted. On a scale from 1-10, my pain level was a consistent 7-8. I could barely walk, and stairs had become almost impossible at that time. I could no longer drive, as the pain from the pressure by placing my foot on either the gas or brake pedal had become almost unbearable. When sitting, the pressure on my spine caused agonizing pain in my back and down both legs. I was in excruciating pain virtually all the time, and the pain medications had little to no effect. The doctor's diagnosis was that I would be paralyzed within two years, and I would have to adapt to a wheelchair.

Was I going to believe the doctors, who prophesied paralysis and a wheelchair, or God's report? God's Report says:

> *"... and **with his stripes** we are healed."* (Isaiah 53:5 bolding mine)

> *"... **by whose stripes** you were healed."* (1 Peter 2:24 bolding mine)

Was I going to believe in God's Report? Asking Father what I should do, His Word to me was, *"Trust Me and start partaking of Communion every day."* I have been faithful to partake of Communion every day as The Lord Commanded, and as a result, I am not paralyzed, nor am I in a wheelchair. The Father continues to touch my body every day. I am walking, sitting, driving, and going up and downstairs because I submit to His Authority and His Healing Power through His Revelation of The Lord's Supper and The Power in The Blood and Body of Jesus Christ, my Lord. The Lord's Supper represents one of the most significant expressions of God's Unconditional Love for you and me.

Our Father also led me to a pain specialist doctor (I pray every day for Divine Connections and Divine Acquaintances, and this doctor was one). Abiding in His Grace, His Strength, and His Ability, I have seen and experienced The Amazing Unconditional Love of our Lord through submission to this doctor and in following his instructions along with prescribed medications. Through the years and the healing process, I have learned and continue to learn and walk where The Holy Spirit Leads me. I continue to walk in faith, believing, and trusting Father for The Manifestation of His total Healing.

During this time, I consciously chose to believe The Report of The LORD, and wherever I have gone (the limitations have been many), I smile and remain as much of my old self as I can. Many people are unaware that I have any problem at all. Several people say things like, "But how could you be in so much pain? You're always smiling." or "You desire prayer? You look so good!"

Here is my point. Too often, we see a person, observe that person, and draw a conclusion based on our intellect. All of this is supported and justified by what we have seen with our physical eyes. Then we make a judgment call because we have reasoned out what we now know and understand the problem (based on what we've seen). Then — we pray and "help God out" by telling Him when and how He is required to fix or repair the problem. Every part of this process has been done with our minds.

What we are imparting when we pray in the understanding of our mind is SELF. We are deceived into thinking and believing that we know exactly what is required. Things we are in danger of imparting when we pray through our minds include rejection, reasoning, bad attitude, deception, distrust, foolishness, doubt, self-reliance, etc.

We impart these things to those we pray for because they are fully aware that we do not know what we are doing. We have not waited on The Holy Spirit to know His Will to pray for them. We are praying according to what our eyes have seen or what the person has said. Therefore, our prayers are a form of manipulation. We are trying to manipulate God into doing what we think they require.

When we pray aloud, those around us learn from what they hear. Therefore, when we pray out of our minds, we impart ignorance, self-reliance, and our own human reasoning. This is no way to teach others how to pray.

Is it any wonder so few people experience effectiveness and power in their prayer lives? Will signs and wonders ever follow our minds? **No**. This is only one of many reasons why we are to have the mind of Christ.

> *"We have the mind of Christ the*
> *Messiah and do hold the thoughts*

(feelings and purposes) *of His heart.*" (1 Corinthians 2:16b AMP)

PRAYING OUR WILL

The will is an inclination, wishing, pleasure, yearning, craving, insistence, commanding, resolution, longing, determination, preference, intention, decisiveness, conviction, and/or control.

Our will represents authority. When we pray out of our will to The Father, what we are saying is: "I am the authority over my life. I know what is best for me and those I love." The attitude of our innermost being is: "I am the delegated authority over this circumstance or situation. I have made a decision and decided what is best for the people in this situation. This is what You should do, how You should do it, and when You should do it. Thank You. Amen."

Sometimes when you pray out of your own will, you are praying as the victim and not the victor. For example, some time ago, I was told of a man and a woman who had separated and were making arrangements for a divorce. They had a little girl, and the grandmother was distraught over this situation.

As it happened, this grandmother knew The Lord and took the matter to prayer. She prayed that this mother and father would reconcile and restore their marriage with all her heart. She could not bear to lose her granddaughter, and she prayed, *"God, please don't let them take away my granddaughter. I can't bear to lose her."* The grandmother's heart was so heavy she would cry for hours on end.

As it turns out, the husband was both an alcoholic and a wife-beater. The wife often had to run out of the house, with her daughter in her arms, searching for a safe place to hide. Unfortunately, the grandmother was not willing to acknowledge or believe this reality.

There are many different viewpoints about marriage and divorce, and it is not my intention to delve into this subject at this time. However, I will say this, our Lord does not expect or desire any person, male or female, young or old, to suffer mental and/or bodily harm at the hand of any individual who is supposed to love them sacrificially. God does not desire any person to be oppressed or incapacitated by fear at any time for any reason.

> *"You were bought at a price; do not become slaves of men."* (1 Corinthians 7:23)

God has not called anyone to live in the spirit of fear and mental instability.

"For God has not given us a spirit of fear, but of power and of love and of a sound mind." (2 Timothy 1:7)

In this case, the root of praying out of her will was fear. The grandmother was praying out of determination and insistence because of the longing and yearning for her granddaughter. The fear of losing her granddaughter prepared her to pray like a victim.

When we pray out of our own will, we will **NEVER** become the victor.

PRAYING OUT OF EMOTIONS

Our emotions are passion, excitement, zeal, elation, joy, grief, remorse, sorrow, shame, depression, hopelessness, despair, fear, inspiration, and/or pride.

Jesus was moved with Compassion. That word means: to be moved as to one's bowels, hence, the phrase, "to be moved with compassion" (for the bowels were thought to be the seat of love and pity.) Some scholars say the bowels were regarded as the seat of more violent passions such as anger and love, but as we learned earlier, the Hebrews believed the bowels to be the seat of the tender affections such as kindness, benevolence, and compassion; hence, the phrase "our heart" (tender mercies, affections, a heart in which mercy resides.)

God's people are often guilty of praying out of sympathy, which is a sameness of feeling, a mutual liking or understanding arising from the sameness of feeling, the ability to enter into another person's mental state, feelings, or emotions.

For example, a person requests prayer for a loved one who has experienced the death of someone very close to them. Because they are emotionally involved, they feel true emotions of grief, sorrow, sympathy, and often great despair for this loved one. So, they may request prayer for this loved one, something like this, "We ask you to pray that Jesus will be close to ______, that He will watch over them, comfort them and give them peace...." Jesus said,

"I will never leave you nor forsake you." (Hebrews 13:5)

With this realization and reality, we then should be praying something to this effect, *"Father, we are asking You to help ______ to see You as they have never seen You before. Please help ______ to know You are there for them, help ______ to know how to reach out to You in this time of pain...."* Wait on The Holy Spirit to see how He Leads you to pray for ______. Jesus Christ has already done The Work on The Cross at Calvary. He has done **ALL** He can. **IT IS FINISHED**. We must now learn how to reach out to Him and receive from Him.

When we pray out of sympathy or emotions, we are praying out of the way we feel. When we pray out of Compassion, we have to get into The Holy Presence of our Lord, experience His heart, and allow The Holy Spirit to pray through us.

WITCHCRAFT PRAYERS

All too often, "witchcraft prayers" go hand in hand with prayers that are prayed out of our emotions. These are petitions and requests out of what we see are required, not what Father's Will is. For example, a believing woman has an unsaved husband. He is out of work and needs to find a job. The bills are piling up. There's a lot of pressure building up in this household. The wife requests prayer at church services, calls the prayer chain and asks for prayer.

The congregation and the prayer teams immediately go to prayer for employment, a new source of income for this man. However, Father Cares even more about this man's soul! You show me one place in Scripture where it is written we are to pray for employment. You cannot find it. It is not there. Of course, Father Cares about the employment situation. However, His Main Concern is the man's eternal destiny.

I have never heard of one person giving their life to Jesus Christ just because they desired to or because it sounded like a good thing to do. No. When I gave my life to Jesus Christ, I was desperate. Most people I talk to have the same story. God got them the easiest way they would come, and it was not easy for some of us.

According to The Word, this woman should be praying something to this effect:

Father, I humbly come before You. I ask for Your Love and Your Mercy for my husband. Thank You that Jesus Christ bore my husband's sins upon The Cross at Calvary. May he see and understand Your Unconditional Love and Your Grace for him and may he believe in and accept Jesus Christ, Your Son, as his Lord and Savior.

I am asking You, Father, to heal my husband's hurts and cause him to see himself as You see him, the wonderful unique individual that You created him to be. Please help me, Father, to show my husband how special he is.

Father, I desire Your heart to love my husband with. I desire to be kind and gentle, to revere my husband and show him the proper honor and respect he deserves. May my husband's heart be softened toward You and the things concerning You. Help me to love him into Your Kingdom.

I desire to be a wife who reflects Your Glory. Please Help me. Above all things, I desire to please Your heart, Father. I require Your Grace, Your Strength, and Your Ability to walk through this difficult time in my life. I choose to trust You, Father, to Protect all my vulnerabilities. You, Father, are my Source, my Provider.

You are aware of our every need. As you take care of Your handmaiden, may my husband's heart be softened, and may he be amazed at Your Supernatural Supply and Your Unconditional Love for our family. Please help me, do this Your Way, to be sensitive to The Holy Spirit, respond to Your leading, and not react out of my flesh.

I know that You have a wonderful purpose and destiny for my husband. I ask You that his destiny will be fulfilled in You. Please fill him full of Your Hope. I also ask that he be Your Blessed and Favored among men. I ask all this in the name of Jesus. Thank You, Father. Amen.

Another gauge that will help you see where your heart is when you pray is to ask yourself these questions:

- Whose requests will be met: the person I am praying for or mine?
- Will my life be easier as the result of this prayer being answered?
- What is the goal?
- What is the root reason I'm praying?
- Where is my heart?
- Am I praying from a selfish motive?
- Am I praying out of concern for the person's well-being?

Witchcraft prayers are when we as individuals have more power and influence over the way we ourselves or other people pray or petition God for whatever the request may be than God does. In other words, we listen to ourselves, or others listen to our instruction rather than go into and search The Word of God for His Instruction or wait on The Holy Spirit for His Instruction.

Soulish and witchcraft prayers are prayed out of all the above feelings rather than or instead of The Will of The Holy Spirit. As a result, they leave us with feelings of fear and doubt.

VARIOUS TYPES OF PRAYERS

PRAYER OF FAITH

> *"And the prayer of faith will save the sick, and the Lord will raise him up. And if he has committed sins, he will be forgiven."* (James 5:15)

PRAYER OF AGREEMENT

> *"Again I say to you that if two of you agree on earth concerning anything that they ask, it will be done for them by My Father in heaven. 20) "For where two or three are gathered together in My name, I am there in the midst of them."* (James 5:15)

PRAYER OF INTERCESSION

"Likewise the Spirit also helps in our weaknesses. For we do not know what we should pray for as we ought, but the Spirit Himself makes intercession for us with groanings which cannot be uttered. 27) *Now He who searches the hearts knows what the mind of the Spirit is, because He makes intercession for the saints **according to the will of God**."* (James 5:15 bolding mine)

PRAYER OF PETITION

"And the king said to Queen Esther, 'The Jews have killed and destroyed five hundred men in Shushan the citadel, and the ten sons of Haman. What have they done in the rest of the king's provinces? Now what is your petition? It shall be granted to you. Or what is your further request? It shall be done.'" (Esther 9:12)

"Again I say to you that if two of you agree on earth concerning anything that they ask, it will be done for them by My Father in heaven. 20) *For where*

two or three are gathered together in My name, I am there in the midst of them." (Matthew 18:19 **&** 20)

"Now this is the confidence that we have in Him, that if we ask anything according to His will, He hears us." (1 John 5:14)

In Closing

In Closing

We have learned that our arch-enemy, satan, tries to rob us of The Blessings of God every day of our lives. However, Jesus Christ, our Lord and Savior, has given us His Armor to wear for His Protection. More than likely, the Apostle Paul learned of The Armor of God from Isaiah 59:14-20.

"Justice is turned back, And righteousness stands afar off; For truth is fallen in the street, And equity cannot enter. 15) *So truth fails, And he who departs from evil makes himself a prey. Then the* LORD *saw it, and it displeased Him That there was no justice.*

16) *He saw that there was no man, And wondered that there was no intercessor; Therefore His own arm brought salvation for Him; And His own righteousness, it sustained Him.* 17) *For He put on righteousness as a breastplate, And a helmet of salvation on His head; He put on the garments of vengeance for clothing, And was clad with zeal as a cloak.* 18) *According to their deeds, accordingly He will repay, Fury to His adversaries, Recompense to His enemies; The coastlands He will fully repay.* 19) *So shall they fear The name of the* LORD *from the west, And His glory from the rising of the sun; When the enemy comes in like a flood, The Spirit of the* LORD *will lift up a standard against him.* 20)

The pieces of God's Armor that Paul encourages us to put on is what The Lord Himself put on to deal vengeance on His adversaries, enforce justice, and protect the righteous. In other words, when you put on The Armor of God, The Lord will repay our arch-enemy, satan, for what he has done to you. Therefore, he, satan, will think twice before he comes against you again.

I urge you to allow God's Truth to shine into every area of your life, and darkness will be put to flight. Walk in The Gift of Righteousness, and you will reign in life.

"For the sin of this one man, Adam, caused death to rule over many. But even greater is God's wonderful grace and his gift of righteousness, for all who receive it will live in triumph over sin and death through this one man, Jesus Christ." (Romans 5:17 NLT)

You can relax. It is possible to live in God's Peace having only a confident expectation of good things to come in your life. Wearing God's Helmet of Salvation assures you of God's Salvation.

Protect yourself with God's Shield, which is faith in His Faith that never fails. Agree with God's Word by speaking it forth, out loud.

Pray in tongues at all times with all perseverance. There will be times when you pray in tongues that you will feel The Power of God! But there will also be times when you feel nothing. When you feel like there is a flow, this is when you persevere. Your arch-enemy, satan, will try to tell you, *"Nothing is happening. You are just making it up. It's nothing but gibberish."* But persevere, and your tongues will flow in His Power.

God has given us His Armor to make us strong in Him and The Power of His Might, so I encourage you to put on God's Armor today and every day of your life.

GOD'S PROVISION IS COMPLETE

I encourage you to remember that it **is ALWAYS ALL ABOUT JESUS** every day of your life. Every Provision that Jesus Christ made for you on The Cross at Calvary is Complete. When you choose — and it is a choice, to wear God's Armor as a lifestyle, His Favor and Blessings will unfold in your daily life. As a result of wearing God's Armor, nothing but good things will happen for you and to you. AMEN.

ABOUT THE AUTHOR

ABOUT THE AUTHOR

Jewell Probasco is a *"practical"* Bible teacher. Her heart desires to teach the Body of Christ how to apply God's Word to their daily lives. The goal is to see each person walk in the Righteousness, Healing, Victory, and Every Inheritance that Jesus Christ sacrificed His life for at The Cross of Calvary.

Jewell has been in the ministry since 1984. She has served in various forms of church leadership, including pastoring, teaching, preaching, counseling, and evangelism in congregations across America. She has ministered at Ministers' Conventions, Women's Ministries, and homes for unwed mothers, to singles, the incarcerated, and with battered and abused women, as well as to congregations. Wherever there are hurting, broken, and wounded people, or just those hungering and thirsting for more of The Truth from God's Word, God has provided opportunities to meet the needs and bring The Gospel in a practical way.

Over the years, God has provided Jewell with many opportunities to share her testimony and the life-changing message of The Gospel of Grace of Jesus Christ. Having her two oldest children taken from her by her ex-husband in 1980, not knowing if they were dead or alive, and realizing she might never see them again, she turned to alcohol as her way to numbness and escape. During those days, her way of life was to consume alcohol from early morning until she would eventually pass out each night. Then in 1982, she met Jesus Christ and gave her life completely over to Him. Through His Power, she was totally delivered and set free. Within two weeks of meeting Jesus, she learned where her children were and had her daughter back in her home within six weeks. Several years later, in June of 2007, she lost her youngest son to suicide. In August of the same year, she learned her middle son did not have long to live. He died in June of the following year, 2008, to a horrible disease. Just like all of us, Jewell also deals with the struggles of everyday life. However, Jewell has discovered the freedom to live victoriously by applying God's Word to her life and desires to help others do the same.

Jewell is an incredible testimony of The Dynamic, Redeeming Work of The Grace of Jesus Christ. Jesus is no respecter of persons. What He did and continues to do for her, He will do for others.

If you have questions or comments, you can contact Jewell at Touchus@masters-touch.us or her website at Masters-Touch.us.

One Last Thing

ONE LAST THING

Amazon gives you the opportunity to rate *'Is It My Armor or God's Armor?'* and share your thoughts *on Facebook and Twitter. If* 'Is It *My Armor or God's Armor?'* has blessed you and you feel it is worth sharing, please would you take a few seconds to let your friends know about it? If it turns out to make a difference in their lives, they'll be forever grateful to you, as will I.

In His Service.
  Jewell

BOOK BY JEWELL PROBASCO

The Power (Ability, Responsibility, and Authority) of Impartation

Looking For Love

The Lord's Supper

Is Tithing For Us Today?

The Gift of Righteousness

10 Reasons Why We Should Give Thanks

A Glimpse of Heaven

The Key To Faith